Published by Periplus Editions with editorial offices at
61 Tai Seng Avenue, #02-12, Singapore 534167

Copyright © 2004 Periplus Editions (HK) Ltd.
All rights reserved.
Hardcover ISBN 978-0-7946-0208-6
Paperback ISBN 978-0-7946-0205-5

Distributed by
North America, Latin America and Europe
Tuttle Publishing, 364 Innovation Drive
North Clarendon, VT 05759-9436 U.S.A.
Tel: 1 (802) 773-8930; Fax: 1 (802) 773-6993
info@tuttlepublishing.com
www.tuttlepublishing.com

Japan
Tuttle Publishing, Yaekari Building, 3rd Floor
5-4-12 Osaki, Shinagawa-Ku, Tokyo 141 0032
Tel: (81) 03 5437-0171; Fax: (81) 03 5437-0755
tuttle-sales@gol.com

Asia Pacific
Berkeley Books Pte Ltd
61 Tai Seng Avenue, #02-12, Singapore 534167
Tel: (65) 6280-1330; Fax: (65) 6280-6290
inquiries@periplus.com.sg
www.periplus.com

Photo credits: All food photography by Luca Invernizzi
Tettoni. Additional photo on page 16 of child eating
noodles by Leong Ka Tai.

Printed in Singapore

hc   10 09 08
       6 5 4 3 2
pb   10 09 08 07 06
       6 5 4 3 2

Contents

Food in China

An ancient, innovative cuisine that is beloved the world over.

China has fascinated the West ever since Marco Polo's account of his travels in that unimaginably exotic land was published in the 13th century. Long before this, however, junks laden with the rich treasures of China had been heading for other countries on annual trading voyages.

Silk, gunpowder, printing and the compass are among the great Chinese inventions that have altered the course of history. But of all China's contributions to modern civilization, the most popular is Chinese food, enjoyed in restaurants and homes in every corner of the globe, from Iceland to Texas to Auckland. Few people in the world, with the possible exception of the French, are as passionately devoted to food as the Chinese. Meals are socially important events and special menus are presented for weddings and birthdays; important festivals also have their traditional dishes and snacks.

What is the reason for the enduring worldwide popularity of Chinese food? It begins with a cornucopia of unique ingredients, vegetables and nourishing tofu, plus subtle or emphatic sauces and seasonings that are partnered with just about every creature that swims the seas, flies the air or roams the land. This astonishing variety of ingredients is transformed by the Chinese into memorable works of culinary art. Every dish must meet three major criteria—appearance, fragrance and flavor; other considerations are texture, the health-giving properties of the food and its auspicious connotations.

The array of seasonings and sauces used by Chinese cooks is not vast; nor are a large range of culinary techniques employed. However, the endless interplay of one basic ingredient with another—meat with tofu, vegetables with slivers of pork, lychees with shrimp—and the transformation of these basics when combined with different seasonings, allows for almost endless variety.

Throughout its history, China has known a perpetual cycle of flood and famine. Food has always been a matter of desperate concern for its huge population (about 25 percent of the world's total population, living on just 7 percent of the world's land). The paradox of Chinese food is that this cuisine, born of hardship and frequent poverty, is not one of dull subsistence, but is arguably the most creative in the world.

You can travel throughout China and the Chinese communities of Asia and never have the same dish served in exactly the same way twice. China's vast territory, diverse population and wide range of regional cuisines provide such infinite variety that eating in this ancient and inventive country is always an enjoyable adventure.

Steamed dumplings are popular in most regions of China, and connoisseurs can recognize their provincial origin by their stuffing and accompanying sauces.

A Rich Culinary Tradition

Early Chinese culinary techniques included boiling, steaming, roasting, stewing, pickling and drying. Stir-frying, the best known method today, probably developed later. In sum, it can be said that the basic Chinese diet and means of preparation were in place about 6,000 years ago, although many imported ingredients—some transported over the Silk Road—entered the Chinese larder and new cooking methods were adopted.

A balanced mixture of grain and cooked dishes has been the ideal of a meal in China since time immemorial. The balance lies between bland, boiled or steamed grain on the one hand, and more flavorful and rich cooked dishes on the other. Further balances were sought between the yin (cooling) and yang (heating) qualities of the foods served. The notion of food as both preventative and curative medicine is deeply imbedded in the Chinese psyche. The specific proportion of grain and cooked dishes on a menu depends as much on the economic status of the diners as on the status of the occasion. Traditionally, grain would provide the bulk of the calories, with cooked dishes serving as supplementary ornamentation and nutrition. The grander the occasion, the more the cooked dishes and the less the grain. Even today, this tradition is maintained at banquets, where a small symbolic bowl of plain steamed rice is served after an extensive selection of other dishes.

Rice is perceived as something essential and almost magical. This is particularly true in South China, while wheat showers its blessings over the North, although this division is not hard and fast. One reason the Grand Canal was built in the 6th century was to transport rice from the fertile Yangtze delta region to the imperial granaries in the relatively dry North. And since the Ming Dynasty (1368–1644), an annual crop of short-grain rice has been grown in the suburbs of Beijing, originally for the palace and today for the military leadership.

Numerous varieties of rice are produced in China today, supplemented by more expensive Thai rice, which is available at urban markets throughout the country. Southerners seem to prefer long-grained rice, which is less sticky than other varieties and has strong "wood" overtones when steaming hot. Rice is served steamed, fried (after boiling) or made into noodles by grinding raw rice into rice flour. It is also cooked with a lot of water to produce congee or *zhou* (rice gruel), a popular breakfast food and late-night snack eaten with a number of savory side dishes.

In early times, wheat was boiled like rice, but by the Han Dynasty (220 B.C.–A.D. 200), the grain was ground into flour and made into noodles, pancakes and various forms of dumplings, some of the recipes having possibly been imported from Central Asia. It is unlikely that Marco Polo brought spaghetti, linguine and pizza to Italy from China. Although their prototypes existed in China centuries before he was born, there is written evidence of the existence of pasta in Italy before Marco Polo left home for the East.

A noted connoisseur of French food complained some forty years ago that all Chinese food tasted "half-cooked." Today, food that is half-raw or half-cooked (the terminology is subjective and interchangeable) seems to be more acceptable, even fashionable, inspired by considerations of health. But who needs the pursuit of longevity as an excuse to enjoy Chinese food?

Diverse Regional Cuisines

It was not so long ago that many Westerners thought of "Chinese food" as a single, homogenous cuisine. However, a country as large and as geographically and climatically varied as China naturally has a wide range of regional cuisines. There is an immense amount of debate, confusion and error about just how many regional cuisines there are, but most knowledgeable gourmets agree that at least four major Chinese regional styles exist: Cantonese, centered on southern Guangdong Province and Hong Kong; Sichuan, based on the cooking of this western province's two largest cities, Chengdu and Chongqing; Huaiyang, the cooking of eastern China—Jiangsu, Zhejiang and Shanghai—an area of lakes, rivers and seashore; and Beijing or "Northern" food, with its major inspiration from the coastal province of Shandong. Some would add a fifth cuisine from the southeastern coastal province of Fujian.

What distinguishes these regional styles is not only their recipes but also the particular types of soy sauce,

garlic, fish, oil, pork or other basic ingredients used in preparing the signature dishes, as well as the proportions of the various ingredients. Timing and temperature are also critical factors. All regions use various forms of ginger, garlic, spring onions, soy sauce, vinegar, sugar, sesame oil and bean paste, but generally combine them in highly distinctive ways.

Delicate Flavors of Cantonese Cooking

Guangdong Province has benefitted from its family ties with freewheeling Hong Kong. The province's fertile soils permit intensive agricultural production and its lengthy shoreline supports a vigorous fishing industry. In a longstanding rivalry with Shanghai, Guangzhou (the provincial capital, once better known to Westerners as Canton) cedes first place in fashion, but is the unchallenged leader when it comes to food.

The earliest Chinese cuisine to be introduced in the West, Cantonese cuisine is often disparagingly identified with egg rolls, chop suey, chow mein, sweet and sour pork and fortune cookies. With the exception of chop suey and fortune cookies, which were invented in the United States, the dishes mentioned above are orthodox Cantonese creations, and sweet and sour pork is just as popular among Chinese as foreigners. But Cantonese cooking has much more to offer than this, and indeed is considered to be the most refined of Chinese cooking styles. Cantonese food is characterized by its extraordinary range and freshness of ingredients, a light touch with sauces and the readiness of its cooks to incorporate "exotic" imported flavorings, such as lemon, curry, Worcestershire sauce and mayonnaise.

Cantonese chefs excel in preparing roast and barbecued meats (duck, goose, chicken and pork), which are never prepared at home (only restaurant kitchens have ovens) and are bought from special roast meat shops.

Cantonese chefs are also famous for *dim sum*, a cooking style in its own right. *Dim sum* refers to snacks taken with tea for either breakfast or lunch. *Dim sum*, which can be sweet, salty, steamed, fried, baked, boiled or stewed, each served in their own individual bamboo steamer or on a plate.

In Cantonese, eating *dim sum* is referred to as *yum cha*, "drinking tea." In traditional *yum cha* establishments, restaurant staff walk about the room pushing a cart or carrying a tray strung around their neck and offer their goods. The mildly competitive shouting only adds to the atmosphere of hustle and bustle. In Hong Kong and Guangzhou, *dim sum* restaurants are important institutions where the locals go to discuss business, read newspapers, raise their children and socialize. At noon and on weekends, getting seats can be difficult as many of them are occupied by "regulars."

LEFT: Inexpensive and delicious street food, such as these dumplings being fried in a Shanghai lane, is enjoyed at least once a day by most Chinese living in towns and cities. RIGHT: Mongolian Lamb Hotpot is popular in winter time and as a reunion dinner, with everyone sitting around in a cozy, warm circle, cooking their own portions of food in the bubbling pot.

Fiery Sichuan Cooking

Sichuan, the home of spicy food, is a landlocked province with remarkably fertile soil and a population of more than 100 million. But despite the province's incendiary reputation, many of the most famous dishes are not spicy at all. For example, the famous duck dish, Camphor and Tea-smoked Duck, is made by smoking a steamed duck over a mixture of tea and camphor leaves.

But it is the mouth-burners (all of them relying on chili peppers for their heat) that have made Sichuan's name known all over the world, dishes like Ma Po Tofu (see page 69), stewed tofu and minced meat in a hot sauce; Hui Guo Rou (see page 82), twice-cooked (boiled and stir-fried) pork with cabbage in a piquant bean sauce; Yu Xiang Qiezi (see page 60), eggplant in "fish flavor" sauce; and fish in hot bean sauce.

Chilies were a relatively late addition to the Sichuan palate, having been imported by Spanish traders in the late Ming or early Qing Dynasty (ca. 1600) from Mexico via the Philippines. The chili's journey on the Pacific Spice Route is a reminder of how plants, as well as ideas, can cross oceans and enrich the lives of the recipients. Sichuan's own taste-tingling spice, Sichuan pepper (the dried berry of an ash tree) still adds its distinctive flavor to many of the province's dishes.

The taste for piquant food is sometimes explained by Sichuan's climate. The fertile agricultural basin is covered with clouds much of the year and there is enough rain to permit two crops of rice in many places. Strong spices provide a pick-me-up in cold and humid weather and are a useful preservative for meat and fish.

When the Grand Canal was built in the Sui Dynasty (A.D. 581–618), it gave rise to several great commercial cities at its southern terminus, including Huaian and Yangzhou, after which this regional cuisine (Huaiyang) is named. The region's location on the lower reaches of the Yangtze River in China's "land of fish and rice" (synonymous with the Western "milk and honey") gave it a distinct advantage in terms of agricultural products, and it was renowned for aquatic delicacies such as fish, shrimp, eel and crab, which were shipped up the canal to the imperial court in Beijing. The cooking of Jiangsu, Zhejiang and Shanghai generally falls into the category of Huaiyang cuisine, which was developed by the great families of the imperially appointed salt merchants living in Yangzhou.

Huaiyang cuisine is not well known outside of China, perhaps because it rejects all extremes and strives for the "Middle Way." Freshness (*xian*) is a key concept in the food of this region, but *xian* means more than just fresh. For example, for a dish of steamed fish to be *xian*, the fish must have been swimming in the tank one hour ago, it must exude its own natural flavor, and must be tender yet slightly chewy.

Xian also implies that the natural flavor of the original ingredients should take precedence over the sauce, and Huaiyang chefs achieve this by careful cutting and paying close attention to the heat of the wok, which is, after all, merely a thin and sensitive membrane of cast iron separating the ingredients from the flames of the stove. Chinese chefs, and Huaiyang chefs in particular, have an uncanny ability to control the flames of their stoves. Some of the best-known Huaiyang dishes are steamed or stewed and thus require less heat and a longer cooking time than most fried dishes; examples include chicken with chestnuts, pork steamed in lotus leaves, duck with an eight-ingredient stuffing, and "lion head" meatballs.

Beijing and the North

The cuisine of Beijing has perhaps been subjected to more outside influences than any other major cuisine in China. First came the once-nomadic Mongols, who made Beijing their capital in the Yuan Dynasty (1279–1368). They brought with them a preference for mutton, the chief ingredient in Mongolian Lamb Hotpot (see page 85), one of Beijing's most popular dishes in the autumn and winter.

And then there were the Manchus, who, as the rulers of the Qing Dynasty (1644–1911), introduced numerous ways of cooking pork. As the capital of China for the last eight centuries, Beijing became the home of government officials who brought their chefs with them when they came from the wealthy southern provinces of Jiangsu and Zhejiang. But the most important influence comes from nearby Shandong Province; in the 19th century, the restaurant industry in Beijing was monopolized by entrepreneurs from Shandong.

LEFT: One of China's most famous dishes, Peking Duck, is traditionally enjoyed three ways: the crisp skin tucked into a pancake smeared with sauce, the meat stir-fried with vegetables, and the carcass made into soup. BELOW: Chicken, duck and pork are roasted in wood-fired ovens in specialty shops and restaurants.

Shandong food has a pedigree that goes back to the days of Confucius, who was a Shandong native. Shandong cuisine features the seafood found along China's eastern seaboard: scallops and squid, both dry and fresh, sea cucumber, conch, crabs, bird's nests and shark's fins. Shandong cuisine is also famous for its use of spring onions and leeks, both raw and cooked.

Beijing's most famous dish, Beijing Roast Duck, owes as much to the culinary traditions of other parts of China as to the capital itself. The ducks, now raised in the western suburbs of Beijing, are said to have swum up the Grand Canal in the wake of imperial grain barges, dining on rice that blew off the boats. The method of roasting the duck is drawn from Huaiyang cuisine, while the pancakes, raw leek and salty sauce that accompany the meat are typical of Shandong.

Beijing is also famous for its steamed and boiled dumplings (*jiaozi*), which are filled with a mixture of pork and cabbage or leeks, or a combination of eggs and vegetables. Dipped in vinegar and soy sauce and accompanied with a nibble of raw garlic, they are one of the simplest but finest pleasures of Chinese cuisine.

Regional cuisine is so popular in China today that in Beijing and Shanghai, for example, there are many more restaurants serving Cantonese and Sichuan food—or advertising that they do—than there are establishments serving local cuisine. Western fast food restaurants have made an impact, but more as a novelty than as a staple of the diet. Chinese food, in all its glory, is here to stay.

All the Tea in China

Tea is a critical ingredient in Chinese life. Tea is drunk before a meal and after a meal, but rarely during a meal. Tea is drunk all day at work, at rest, when alone or with friends. Indeed, it is hard to imagine a situation in which tea is not present. Tea drinking is a Chinese invention, although the plant may have first been grown in Southeast Asia. In any case, the written record suggests that tea has been cultivated and drunk in China since the Han Dynasty (220 B.C.–A.D. 200).

The Japanese tea ceremony, which makes use of powdered tea and a bamboo brush to beat the tea until a froth appears on the surface, was inspired by Chinese tea customs in the Tang Dynasty. But the custom of drinking steeped leaf tea, as we know it today, began only during the Ming Dynasty (1368–1644). This accompanied the emergence of fine white porcelain that showed off the color and shape of the leaves to their best advantage.

There is only one tea plant, but many types of tea. Variations in color and flavor are obtained by the picking, fermentation, rolling and roasting time. Generally speaking, there are three types of tea: unfermented green tea, such as Longjing (Dragon Well); semi-fermented tea, such as Oolong; and fermented tea, such as the "black tea" (in Chinese, it is called "red tea") most popular in India and the West. Green tea is further mixed with jasmine blossoms to make jasmine tea, a favorite summer drink in North China. In South China, from Guangdong west to Yunnan, musty-rusty Pu'er tea is the most common drink.

Tea can be steeped in a pot or a cup. Fastidious drinkers discard the first, brief steeping as a way of cleaning the leaves and dilating them for the second steeping, regarded by many as the best. Good tea can be steeped as many as ten times. Judging from wine vessels found in archeological sites, it is likely that wine was first made in China from grain using the method of yeast fermentation around 5,000 years ago, when it was offered to the God of the Sun and the ancestors in rituals. The technique of distilling wine from kaoliang, a form of sorghum, became popular around 800 years ago.

The leading Chinese-style grain wines are classified as either "white" (*bai jiu*) or "yellow" (*huang jiu*). White wines are distilled spirits with an alcohol content ranging from 40 to 60 percent. The most famous brand of white—more accurately, clear—spirits is Maotai, made in the southwest province of Guizhou. These potent drinks are usually taken "straight up" in small cups or glasses during a meal.

Yellow wine, distilled from glutinous rice, is produced in the coastal area near Shanghai. The most famous source is Shaoxing, in Zhejiang Province. Yellow wine has an alcohol content of approximately 14 percent and is often compared to dry sherry. It is frequently used in cooking and imparts a rich, yeasty flavor to fish and many other dishes.

The history of beer brewing in China goes back more than a century to the German concession in Qingdao (or Tsingtao), on the coast of Shandong Province. Qingdao is still home to the largest brewery in China today. Believe it or not, three billion beer bottles circulate freely among the breweries in China, and a bottle of beer costs no more than 25 cents.

Since 1990, food markets in China have been flooded with bottled mineral water; at present there are over 1,000 "sources" throughout the country. Several companies have also started selling distilled and filtered drinking water, yet another sign of the rising standard of living in China.

Chinese (understandably) never drink unboiled tap water. The strong chlorine taste in most city water—particularly in the Shanghai area where much of the drinking water is taken from the Yangtze and has a muddy fragrance as well—makes these bottled waters a welcome change, particularly for making tea, soup, rice and noodles.

ABOVE: A surprising range of wines and spirits are found in special wine shops in China's towns and cities. Cooking wines made from glutinous rice are found in regular provision shops. LEFT: Tea is more than just a drink in China, and the teahouse, where men gather to gossip, occupies much the same social role as a pub in England or a bar in France. OPPOSITE: Three generations sit down to a meal in the courtyard of an old house in Fujian Province, southern China.

The Emperor's Banquet

As the Son of Heaven, the emperor of China enjoyed a status so elevated above the common mortal that it is difficult to conceive of the awe in which he was held and the power that he enjoyed. In the realm of food, however, the emperor was subject to numerous restrictions.

The emperor could, however, take his meals at any time and in any place. In fact, there were no dining rooms per se in the Forbidden City; tables were set up before the emperor whenever and wherever he decided to eat.

Every meal was a banquet of approximately 100 dishes. These included 60 or 70 dishes from the imperial kitchens, and a few dozen more served by the chief concubines from their own kitchens. For reasons of security, however, the emperor could not order a specific dish lest it be poisoned the next time it was served. Nor could he express a positive opinion about any particular dish. Security was monitored by inserting a silver rod into each dish, which would turn black if it came into contact with arsenic. At every meal the emperor dined off museum-quality porcelain, with gold, silver, jade, rhinoceros horn, lacquer tableware and chopsticks. Many of the dishes were made purely for their visual appeal and were placed far away from the reach of the imperial chopsticks. These leftovers were spirited out of the palace to be sold to gourmets eager to "dine with the emperor".

Fastidious records were kept in the imperial kitchen, which had over 100 woks, with three men assigned to each. The names of each dish made by the chefs and the amount of ingredients used were recorded. At one imperial banquet held on the eve of Chinese New Year in 1784, the emperor Qianlong was personally served a total of about 150 kilograms of meat, including 3 ducks, 10 chickens, 6 pheasants, 5 geese, 12 kilograms of boar, 10 kilograms of mutton, 10 kilograms of fish, and 4 deer's tails—a fit repast for any emperor!

Today, Fangshan and Listening to the Orioles Pavilion are two restaurants in Beijing, specialize in dishes said to be prepared according to authentic imperial recipes.

LEFT: The last Dowager Empress of China may well have dined in this very spot, on the edge of the lake in the gardens of the Summer Palace outside Beijing.
RIGHT: An old Chinese painting depicting an obviously important and wealthy Chinese gentleman being entertained by a woman playing music, while being tempted with a range of delicacies.

Home and Market

The proliferation of refrigerators in China today is making inroads on an institution that for centuries has been an essential part of daily life, that is, shopping in the local food market. Quite unwittingly, markets in China make excellent destinations for tourists, sociologists and economists. Here, one can observe the locals squeezing fruit—and fruit sellers squeezing the customers—and the high-pitched haggling that revolves around the price of a fistful of pork which costs less than a penny, but where loss of face is at stake. You may also observe how the emerging middle class and nouveaux riche interact with the food sellers, who are usually of peasant origin.

Most dealers have their regular customers and try to please them by throwing in the extra strawberry or potato or backing off on the price, every now and then. With six people selling exactly the same cucumbers, tomatoes and string beans within earshot, competition is fierce.

Many men and women go to the market two or three times a day. In some state-run offices in Beijing, for example, half-hour rest periods are allotted for shopping for lunch and dinner. Although prices are not marked on most stands, the average housewife knows the price of every item in the market and what she paid two weeks ago. Food in China may appear inexpensive compared to the West, but food purchases consume 40–60 percent of the average household budget, as rent for many is negligible.

In addition to fresh food markets, there are shops selling a huge variety of prepared and packaged food, which can be fascinating for the first-time visitor. China's open policy since 1978 has resulted in what the locals call, "100 flowers blooming" in the area of comestibles, particularly in the

major cities, where people have more disposable time and cash than before.

Along with food markets, most cities have areas where snack foods are sold in stand-up or sit-down stalls. Breakfast is well-catered for in almost every city, as the morning meal is the one people are most likely to eat outside the home or work place. Popular breakfasts are: a fried egg wrapped in a pancake; an "elephant ear", which is a plate-sized piece of fried bread; noodles; congee (rice gruel) or tofu jelly accompanied by a deep-fried cruller (*you tiao*); or a slice of cake and a jar of milk.

Every region has its own particular snacks, very often sold on the street. Snack food is very inexpensive and includes such regional specialties as Beijing's boiled tripe with fresh coriander, fried starch sausage with garlic, sour bean soup, and boiled pork and leek dumplings (*jiaozi*).

Shanghai is known for its steamed *baozi* dumplings and sweet glutinous rice with eight sweetmeats (*babaofan*). Sichuan is noted for spicy *dan dan* noodles, dumplings in hot sauce and tofu jelly (*dou hua*), while Cantonese *dim sum* is a cuisine unto itself.

The average urban family eats its main meal of the day in the evening. This meal usually consists of a staple such as rice or noodles, one or two fried dishes, at least one of which contains meat or fish, and a soup. Beer regularly accompanies meals at home. Cramped quarters make it difficult for home cooking to be fancy, but Sunday provides a good excuse for moderate culinary excesses. The whole family gets involved in the business of shopping and cooking, and friends or relatives may be invited to join in the feast. For the vast bulk of the population, it is rice and vegetables, the way Mother used to make it.

Cooking and Eating Chinese

Perhaps the most surprising aspect of a Chinese kitchen is its utter simplicity. It's hard to believe that such creative and often sophisticated food is prepared with so few utensils. Even today, most cooks manage with a single coal-fired stove, which in China, is basically a bench top with several holes of differing sizes where woks, claypots and saucepans are placed.

Indispensible Utensils
The most essential ingredient is a **wok**, a parabolic pan traditionally made of cast iron and used for just about everything except cooking rice: stir-frying, deep-frying, braising, making sauces, holding a steaming basket and so on. The shape of the wok distributes the heat evenly, while its sloping sides ensure that during stir-frying, food falls back into the pan and not out over the edge. It's also practical for deep-frying, requiring less oil than a conventional saucepan or frying pan.

A wok should be "seasoned" before its first use so that food will not stick to it. Wash the inside of the wok with warm, soapy water but do not use a scouring pad. Rinse with fresh water and dry thoroughly. Place some oil on a piece of paper towel and wipe the inside of the wok. Repeat two or three times until the paper towel comes away clean after wiping. Store the oiled wok until you are ready to use it. Before cooking, Chinese cooks always heat the wok before adding any oil to ensure that it is dry and the oil will not splatter. After cooking, never clean your wok with detergent or harsh abrasives; just rinse with warm water and wipe it dry.

Claypots of various shapes and sizes, with a sandy exterior and a glazed interior, are used for slow cooking and for making soups and stocks. These are attractive and inexpensive, but any type of **saucepan** could be used instead. Rice is usually cooked in an aluminium or stainless steel saucepan, although more and more affluent homes in the cities boast an **electric rice cooker**.

Just as indispensable as the wok is a cleaver, which comes with either a heavy rectangular blade about 3 to 4 inches deep, ideal for cutting through bones, or a lighter weight blade for chopping, slicing, bruising garlic cloves and scooping up food on the flat edge to carry it to the pan. One single **Chinese cleaver** does the work of a whole battery of knives in a Western kitchen.

Partner to the cleaver is a strong **chopping board**, which in China, is a thick cross section of a tree trunk.

Meat is always minced on a board, using two cleavers simultaneously—a **food processor** achieves similar results without the effort and skill that is required to use two cleavers.

Steaming is a healthy method of cooking favored by the Chinese, who traditionally use a multi-tiered **bamboo steamer** with a woven cover that absorbs any moisture, unlike a metal cover where moisture condenses and then falls back onto the food. The steaming basket is placed inside a wok, sitting a few inches above the boiling water. Chinese stores also sell perforated metal disks that sit inside a wok above the water level; these are useful for steaming a single plate of food. For steaming in this fashion, you will need to buy a large, dome-shaped lid that will cover your wok.

Other useful utensils include a **wire mesh basket** on a long handle, good for scooping out deep-fried food or boiled noodles; and a **round-edged frying spatula**, which is perfect for tossing stir-fried ingredients in the wok. Chinese cooks also prefer **long wooden chopsticks** for turning food during deep-frying, though this does require a certain dexterity, and you may be happier with tongs.

Simple Cooking Methods
Cooking methods include steaming, stir-frying, braising, deep-frying and slow cooking.

Stir-frying is by far the most commonly used method. Oil is heated in the wok and evenly sliced ingredients tossed about constantly; contact with the heat from the sides as well as the bottom of the wok means that food cooks very rapidly, sealing in the juices and flavor.

OPPOSITE: This Chinese kitchen has the traditional coal-fired stove in the corner, as well as a modern two-burner gas cooker. LEFT: A wok, the most essential item in a Chinese kitchen. ABOVE: Chinese claypots, used for slow cooking, are attractive and inexpensive. BELOW: A bamboo steamer and long-handled wire mesh scoops.

Timing is absolutely crucial to the success of Chinese dishes. Most food is cooked very briefly (a result of centuries of having to conserve precious fuel), so it is essential to chop all the ingredients, measure all the seasonings, and have the garnishes and serving dishes at hand before starting to cook.

Control of heat is also important, and for this reason, a gas flame is far superior to any other form of heat. The degree of heat required for some dishes, especially for stir-frying, is far greater than that normally used in a Western kitchen.

Timing given in the recipes in this book assumes that very high heat can be used when called for; if you doubt the intensity of your heat source, try cooking the food for just a little longer. If you have an electric stove, you might consider investing in a single gas burner capable of producing extremely high heat and of immediate temperature control, otherwise your results will not be the same.

One single wok can be used to cook the entire meal, except for the rice. The first dish is cooked, the wok quickly rinsed with water, dried and the next batch of ingredients added. Naturally, the Chinese cook doesn't have to break off in the middle of cooking to check the recipe. Make sure you prepare and place the ingredients near your stove in order of use so you can work as quickly as possible, and have your serving plates ready. And remember, as any Chinese cook would agree, practice makes perfect.

Chinese Dining Etiquette 101

Don't point with your chopsticks, and don't stick your chopsticks into your rice bowl and leave them there standing up, for in this position they resemble incense sticks set before a grave.

Don't use your chopsticks to explore the contents of a dish. Locate the morsel you want—on top of the pile, not buried in the middle of it—with your eyes and go directly for it with your chopsticks without touching any other pieces. A wait-and-see-attitude is recommended if you wish to land the white meat, the wing or the chicken heart.

If you wish to take a drink of wine at a formal dinner, you must first toast another diner, regardless of whether he or she responds by drinking. If you are toasted and don't wish to drink, simply touch your lips to the edge of the wine glass to acknowledge the courtesy.

It is incumbent upon the host to urge the guests to eat and drink to their fill. This means ordering more food than necessary and keeping an eye out for idle chopsticks. It is polite to serve the guest of honor the best morsels, such as the cheek of the fish, using a pair of serving or "public" chopsticks, or with the back end of one's chopsticks.

If you have had enough to eat, yet your host still plies you with food, or if you do not wish to indulge in fish lips, sea cucumber or duck web, graciously allow your host to place the delicacy on your plate; leaving food uneaten indicates you do not care for it. It is socially acceptable in China to spit bones on the table, belch, slurp soup and noodles and smoke while eating.

Rice can be eaten by raising the bowl to the mouth and shoveling the grains in with the chopsticks in a rapid fanning motion, even though this may resemble a Beijing duck force-feeding itself.

Chinese banquets commonly have 12 to 20 courses in succession and can last for hours, but the dinner is over when the host stands up and offers the final toast; one is expected to leave immediately thereafter. Chatting at the table over coffee after a meal, or retiring to the drawing room is not part of Chinese etiquette.

RIGHT: A selection of fresh and dried noodles. In some areas of China, fresh hand-pulled noodles are still prepared today. BELOW: An oil pot for drizzling oil into the wok is an attractive option. ABOVE LEFT: This child seems more concerned with eating than etiquette, but will no doubt pick up the finer points of dining as he grows up.

Authentic Chinese Ingredients

A trip to an Asian market is a must to stock up on hard-to-get items, however, many Chinese ingredients are now available in supermarkets and health food stores.

Azuki beans, or red beans, are small dried beans often used in desserts. They are also cooked with sugar to make sweet red bean paste, which is sold in cans or jars. The dried beans and paste are sold in Asian markets.

Bitter gourd is also known as bitter melon, bitter cucumber and balsam pear. It is a green, ridged vegetable with a white flesh that is native to China. It is, as its name suggests, slightly bitter in taste. Choose young, green bitter gourd—the deeper the green, the younger the bitter gourd. Look in Asian markets.

Bok choy is a highly nutritious variety of cabbage with long, crisp stalks and spinach-like leaves. It has a clean, slightly peppery flavor and is a wonderful addition to soups and stir-fries. **Baby bok choy** are the small, tender variety of bok choy. Bok choy is available in most well-stocked supermarkets.

Bamboo shoots are the fresh shoots of the bamboo plant and make an excellent vegetable. Fresh shoots taste better than canned, but must be peeled, sliced and simmered in water for about 30 minutes before using. Ready-to-use sliced bamboo shoots, packed in water, can be found in the refrigerated produce section of some supermarkets and are convenient and easy to use. Canned bamboo shoots should be boiled for 5 minutes to reduce any metallic flavor before using. Both fresh and canned bamboo shoots are increasingly available in many supermarkets.

Bean sprouts are sprouted from a number of beans, but mung bean sprouts are the most common type of sprout found in the produce section of most supermarkets. Store them in the refrigerator, covered with water, where they will keep for 2 to 3 days. Many Chinese cooks remove the split bean heads and tails before cooking, but this is optional. Wash the sprouts thoroughly before cooking.

Black Chinese mushrooms, also known as shiitake mushrooms, are large and meaty, and are used in many recipes throughout this book. Fresh shiitake are increasingly available in supermarkets although porcini mushrooms, or dried black Chinese mushrooms may be used as well. If using dried mushrooms, soak in hot water for 10 to 15 minutes to soften, then drain and discard the stems before dicing or slicing the caps.

Black vinegar is made from rice, wheat and millet, or sorghum. The best black vinegars are well-aged and have a complex, smoky flavor. Chinese cooks add black vinegar sparingly to sauces, dips and when braising meats. Balsamic vinegar is a good substitute.

Blended mustard is made up of ground brown and white mustard seeds mixed with wine, vinegar, or water and various spices such as tumeric. Colman's mustard powder, available in most supermarkets, is a good choice although it is milder than the pure mustard normally served in Chinese restaurants. Japanese mustard is an acceptable substitute.

Boxthorn berries are oval-shaped red berries, also known as wolfberries. They are prized for their medicinal properties and are available dried from Chinese apothecaries and in Asian markets.

Chicken stock powder is made up of loose granules of chicken stock, used to add extra flavor to dishes. This powder can be quite salty, so be sure to taste the dish before adding any salt. Substitute with instant chicken broth mix or bouillon cubes. Most supermarkets sell the various forms of chicken stock.

Chili oil is made from dried chilies or chili powder steeped in oil, which is used to flavor some Sichuan dishes. Bottled chili oil is also available in Asian markets, or you can make your own with the following recipe:

3/4 cup (175 ml) peanut oil
1 tablespoon Sichuan peppercorns
2 dried chilies, sliced

Heat a wok or frying pan and add the oil, peppercorns and chilies. Cook over low heat for 10 minutes, then cool and store in a glass container for 2 to 3 days. Strain and discard the peppercorns and chilies. Store in an airtight glass jar and keep in a cool place for up to 6 months.

Chili paste consists of ground fresh chilies, sometimes mixed with other ingredients such as vinegar, garlic or black beans, and commonly sold in jars. The heat may vary from brand to brand, depending on the ingredients that are added to the paste. Sichuan chili paste is made from dried chilies that are soaked in water and then ground to a paste in a spice grinder or food processor with a touch of oil. You can make your own and store it in the refrigerator, or purchase ready-made chili paste in Asian markets and well-stocked supermarkets.

Chinese broccoli, also known as *kailan* or Chinese kale, has long, narrow stems and leaves, and small edible flowers. The stems are the tastiest part while the leaves are slightly bitter and are often discarded. Chinese broccoli is available fresh in Asian markets. Substitute with broccoli stems, bok choy or broccolini.

Chinese cabbage, also known as Napa cabbage, has white stems that end in tightly packed pale green leaves. It has a mild, delicate taste.

Chinese chives are also known as garlic chives, and have a garlic flavor and aroma. Unlike the Western chives, which have rounded stems, Chinese chives have long, thin stems, and resemble flat spring onions. Chinese chives can be found in Asian markets and many gourmet produce markets. Regular Western chives are an acceptable substitute.

Chinese preserved plum has a strong, sweet-salty taste with a slightly sour undertone, and is packed in salted rice vinegar. Scrapings of the flesh are used to make plum sauce. Both the preserved plums and the sauce are available in Asian markets.

Chinese sausage, or *lap cheong*, is a sweet pork sausage that is dried and often colored red. It can be found hanging in bunches, or in plastic packets in Asian markets. Substitute with sweet Italian sausage.

Daikon radish is a large, crisp, white-fleshed radish, with a sweet and clean flavor. It is a vegetable that is widely used in Japanese and Korean cooking, and can be eaten raw, or cooked. The skin needs to be peeled or scrubbed before using. Daikon is available from Asian markets and any well-stocked supermarket.

Dried shrimp are used to season many dishes, particularly sauces. They can be small or large; the better quality ones are bright orange in color and shelled. They should be soaked in warm water for 10 minutes before adding to a recipe. Dried shrimp are often sold in vacuum sealed plastic bags in Asian markets.

Five-spice powder contains a mixture of ground spices usually consisting of equal parts of cinnamon, cloves, fennel seed, star anise and Sichuan peppercorns. Five-spice powder is available prepared in the supermarket.

Ginseng is a highly prized medicinal root, sometimes used in cooking, which is thought to convey longevity. The root is sold in Chinese apothecaries and can be quite expensive, but packets of less costly root hairs or shavings may be purchased in most Asian food stores. Pure ginseng tea bags are also widely available.

Glutinous rice flour is a very fine white flour made from glutinous rice. It has a sticky texture that lends itself well to pastries and sweets. It is usually sold in plastic packets in Asian markets.

Hoisin sauce consists of fermented soybeans, garlic, chilies, and vinegar. The sauce is thick and dark and has as sweet, salty flavor. Commercially bottled or canned hoisin sauce is available in most grocery stores.

Lotus is a water lily whose root and seeds are widely eaten and used in Asian cooking. **Lotus root** has a cruchy texture and a beautiful lacy pattern when sliced crosswise. The long roots are sold fresh in Asian grocery stores, often wrapped in dried mud to keep them moist and are also available frozen and pre-sliced in plastic packets, or canned. Fresh lotus must be peeled before using. Substitute fresh lotus root with jicama. Delicately flavored **lotus seeds** are available both fresh, dried and canned from Asian grocery stores. Dried seeds should be soaked in boiling water for 1 hour, then peeled, and the bitter, green core in the middle of the seed removed and discarded. Canned lotus seeds normally have this bitter core already removed.

Lychees are small red fruit with a knobbly red shell, encasing sweet, white translucent flesh that is similar in texture to a grape. Both the shell and the seed need to be removed before use. Fresh lychees are usually available in Asian markets, but if you can't find them, the canned variety in sweet syrup is a good substitute. The syrup can be used as a sweetener, in place of sugar.

Noodles are available in many forms, and are made from either rice, wheat or mung bean flour. Dried **rice vermicelli** are very fine rice threads that must be soaked before using. **Egg noodles**, like pasta, are made from wheat flour, water and egg. They are available both fresh and dried and should not be overcooked as the recipe may call for the egg noodles to be stir-fried after they are softened in boiling water. Substitute egg noodles with **ramen noodles**, which are dried Chinese-style wheat noodles. They are most commonly available in the form of instant noodles and available in plastic packets in well-stocked supermarkets. There are other varieties of wheat flour noodles that are also available fresh and dried, from Asian grocery stores. Both fresh and dried noodles need to be dropped into boiling water before using—use a pair of long chopsticks to separate the noodles while they are cooking, to prevent them from sticking together.

Oyster sauce is a flavorful soy-based sauce made with oyster extract: a Cantonese specialty. A vegetarian version is available, and is sometimes sold as "mushroom oyster sauce" or "oyster-flavored sauce". If you do not like monosodium glutamate, choose your brand carefully as most are laden with this additive. Oyster sauce is available in most supermarkets. Soy sauce or Worcestershire sauce may be substituted although the flavor will not be the same.

Preserved salted radish or *chai poh* is pickled Japanese radish or daikon. Often added to dishes for its crunchy texture and salty flavor, it keeps almost indefinitely and is available at Asian markets. The Japanese version may be substituted.

Rice flour wrappers are made from rice flour, water and salt. These wrappers are already cooked and unlike spring roll wrappers, do not need to be deep-fried or cooked any further. They are used to enclose a variety of fresh fillings and are available in Asian markets. Look for *popiah* wrappers or *moo-shu* pancakes.

Rice wine adds a sweet, subtle flavor to dishes. It also acts as a tenderizer, blending and enhancing flavors. It is widely available in Asian markets and the specialty food section of some supermarkets. Sake or dry sherry are good substitutes.

Salted black beans are also called fermented black beans and Chinese black beans. They are soybeans that have been fermented and preserved in salt, hence their strong, salty flavor. Mainly used to season a number of dishes, especially fish, beef and chicken, they are sold in packets or cans and can be kept for several months if stored in the refrigerator. Soak in warm water for 30 minutes before using, to remove excess salt.

Salted mustard cabbage (*mei cai*) is the Chinese equivalent of sauerkraut. The salted mustard greens are sold in a jar for use as a dip or to add hot and spicy flavor to a dish. It is normally sold in sealed plastic bags, which can keep for several months if unopened. Once the package has been opened, the cabbage can be stored refrigerated in an airtight container for about 6 months. Before using, salted mustard cabbage should be soaked and rinsed in several changes of water to remove excess saltiness.

Sesame paste is made from ground toasted sesame seeds, unlike the Middle Eastern equivalent (tahini) which is made from untoasted seeds. Sesame paste is available in cans and jars in Asian markets. Substitute smooth peanut butter.

Sichuan peppercorns are not really pepper, but a round, reddish-brown berry with a pronounced fragrance and acidic flavor, used primarily in Sichuan cuisine and as an ingredient in five-spice powder. Unfortunately, Sichuan peppercorns may be hard to come by in the US as their import was banned by the Department of Agriculture. You may be lucky to find some in a well-stocked Asian market or Chinatown. Japanese *sansho* pepper, sold in small bottles, contains other ingredients, but has a similar flavor.

Sichuan pickles, or *zha cai*, are made with purple and green kohlrabi that is preserved in vinegar and spiced with ginger and chili. They are tender-crisp and have a hot, sour, salty taste. They add piquancy to stir-fries and other dishes when used as an ingredient, and make a delicious side dish. Many Chinese cooks make their own pickles, but they are also available in jars at Asian markets.

Soy sauce is a very important condiment in Asian cooking. It is a dark, salty sauce made by fermenting boiled soybeans and roasted wheat or barley. Although there is essentially one main type of soy sauce widely made in the US, Asian countries such as China, Korea and Japan produce a number of varieties ranging in color from light to dark and in texture from thin to thick. Chinese **black soy sauce** is extremely dark and thick. It has a much richer flavor and color due to the addition of molasses. Japanese tamari can be substituted.

Spring roll wrappers are thin sheets of light, pliable pastry made from wheat flour, eggs and salt. These wrappers are usually used to wrap a variety of fillings, then deep-fried until golden brown. They are available both fresh and frozen in well-stocked supermarkets and Asian markets. They are also sold in the West as egg roll wrappers, and are often called skins, rather than wrappers in Asia. Indonesian or Filipino lumpia skins are good substitutes.

Star anise is a brown, star-shaped spice with eight points, each containing a shiny seed that has a pronounced aniseed flavor. Often used whole and cooked with beef, it is available in plastic packets in the spice section of Asian markets and well-stocked supermarkets.

Straw mushrooms are grown on straw used in paddy fields, hence their name. They are small, tan mushrooms with compact caps, thin stems and have a musty, earthy flavor. These mushrooms are a popular addition to Asian soups and stir-fries. Often available in open air markets throughout Asia, in the West, straw mushrooms are mostly available canned in supermarkets, or dried, in Asian markets.

Tapioca pearls are tiny beads made from cassava starch. The uncooked pearls are hard and white when dried, but turn soft and translucent when cooked. Tapioca pearls are often used in desserts and to thicken dough. The pearls are sold in plastic packets in Asian markets.

Tofu, or bean curd, is available in various textures ranging from silken to firm. **Firm tofu** holds its shape when cut or cooked and has a stronger, slightly sour taste. **Pressed tofu** (which confusingly is often labeled as "firm tofu") has much of the moisture extracted and is therefore much firmer in texture than normal tofu—it is commonly eaten in Asia as a meat substitute. **Soft** or **silken tofu** is slippery and tends to crumble easily, but has a silky texture and refined flavor. Soft tofu is available packed in square plastic boxes or shaped into cylinders and wrapped in plastic. **Tofu skin** is the thin, rich layer of soy protein that forms on the surface of soy milk while it is being boiled to make tofu. The skin that is formed is then dried and sold in long, thin strips or rectangular sheets. It has a wonderful chewy texture and flavor. **Tofu skin wrappers** are also made from dried tofu skin and are large, folded, opaque sheets that are light brown in color and often used to wrap spring rolls and other fillings. Tofu skin is available in plastic packets in Asian markets and the various forms of tofu can be found in any well-stocked supermarket.

Water chestnuts are small, acorn-shaped roots with a brown leathery skin outside and a crisp, crunchy flesh and a juicy sweet flavor inside. Fresh water chestnuts can be found packed in water in the refrigerated sections of some supermarkets. Canned water chestnuts are also available.

Winter Melon is a member of the squash family. The white flesh has a mild flavor and is delicious in stir-fries and soup. Winter melon is available year-round in Chinese markets and specialty produce stores. Substitute with peeled and deseeded cucumber, or zucchini.

Wood ear mushrooms are also called wood ear fungus, and are tree mushrooms that have a crunchy texture and a delicate woodsy flavor. They are available both fresh and dried in Chinese markets and are dark brown to black in color. Soak dried mushrooms in hot water until soft. Substitute with shiitake mushrooms.

Wonton wrappers are made from wheat dough, and come in a variety of sizes and thicknesses. They are filled with meat or vegetables, then steamed, fried or used in soups. Fresh or frozen wonton wrappers are available in most supermarkets.

White vinegar is made from glutinous rice and has a mild, sweet flavor. It is colorless and is one of the definitive ingredients used in sweet and sour sauce. Substitute with Japanese rice vinegar or white wine vinegar.

Authentic Chinese Recipes

Planning a Chinese meal
The Chinese typically eat family-style. A "typical" Chinese meal will start with a pickle and one or two appetizers (like Pork Dumplings in Hot Sauce or Classic Egg Rolls), followed by a soup, a meat or poultry dish, a seafood dish, and a vegetable dish. The main courses are usually accompanied by white rice. Fried noodles might be added if there are more than 6 people, however, fried noodles and rice dishes are more commonly eaten as the centerpiece of a casual lunch or dinner, with one or two appetizers, or vegetables. Dipping sauces are normally served with each main dish and placed on the table for people to help themselves. As a general rule, the recipes in this book will serve 4–6 people as part of a meal with rice or soup, and three other main dishes.

Shopping for ingredients
Select the freshest possible ingredients. Most of the dishes in this book are just briefly cooked and some of them are only lightly seasoned. Using high quality ingredients ensures that the fresh, pure taste of the food shines through.

Preparation
It is of utmost importance to clean, cut and measure out all of the ingredients required for a recipe ahead of time. Stir-frying is a quick cooking method that leaves very little time to measure out condiments and prepare meat and vegetables during cooking. Taking the time to prepare the ingredients will help you succeed when trying the recipes.

Tips for deep-frying
When deep-frying, use enough oil and ensure that the food is submerged completely. Heat the oil to 350–375°F (180–190°C), or until a small piece of ingredient bubbles when dropped into the oil. Be sure to slide small amounts of foods into the wok to prevent splattering. Foods to be deep-fried should be dry and at room temperature to reduce the drop in the temperature of the oil when you add them. Use a wire basket, or very long bamboo chopsticks to remove the items from the oil. Keep the oil hot and do not overcrowd the wok, and your food will turn out light and crispy.

Tips for steaming
Line your bamboo steamer with cabbage leaves when steaming wontons, rice dumplings or any other glutinous foods, and be sure not to overcrowd the steamer to prevent the foods from sticking.

Caring for your wok
Carbon steel woks are among the best and cheapest of woks, but they require a bit of care. To clean one, set it over high heat and scrape any bits from the sides using a wooden spatula. Add a couple of cups of water and continue to remove loosened bits with the spatula. When sufficiently clean, pour out the water, then rinse and dry thoroughly. Since rust is the enemy, set the cleaned wok back on the stove over medium heat for a minute or two to ensure that it is completely dry. Lastly, grease the inside of the wok with some cooking oil, making sure you cover all the surface area with oil. This will prevent the wok from rusting.

Pickles and Relishes

Hunan Chili Relish

5 red and 5 green chilies
5 cloves garlic
1 medium onion
1 tablespoon oil
$^1/_4$ teaspoon salt

1 Coarsely chop the chilies, garlic and onion. Heat the oil and stir-fry the chopped ingredients for 1 minute. Add the salt and serve warm, or at room temperature as an appetizer, or as an accompaniment to fried rice.

Preparation time: 5 mins
Cooking time: 1 min   Yields: 2 cups

Pickled Daikon and Carrot

1 small daikon radish, peeled
1 medium carrot, peeled
2 teaspoons salt
1 fresh red chili, deseeded
2 tablespoons sugar
2 tablespoons white vinegar

1 Cut the daikon and carrot into small slices, or matchstick pieces of equal sizes, then place in a bowl and sprinkle with salt, stirring to mix well. Leave for 15 minutes, then squeeze to remove the moisture. Cut the chili into very fine lengthwise shreds and add, together with the sugar and vinegar, to the daikon and carrot. Chill before serving.

Preparation time: 20 mins + chilling time
Yields 3 cups

Pickled Green Chili

1 cup (250 ml) white vinegar
8 green chilies, sliced
$1/2$ teaspoon salt

1 Bring $1/2$ cup (125 ml) of the white vinegar to a boil in a medium saucepan, add the chilies and boil for 15 seconds. Drain and discard the vinegar.
2 Place the chilies, remaining vinegar, and salt in a dry, glass jar. Cover and leave to marinate overnight before serving with noodle dishes, or as a relish.

Preparation time: 5 mins + overnight marinating time   Cooking time: 5 mins
Yields 2 cups

Marinated Broccoli Stems

Broccoli stems from 2 heads of
  broccoli
1 cup (250 ml) water
1 teaspoon salt
1 star anise pod
Pinch of dried chili flakes (optional)

1 Peel the broccoli stems and cut into strips. Combine the broccoli stems with all the other ingredients and marinate for 8 hours. Drain and serve as an appetizer.

Preparation time: 10 mins + 8 hours marinating time   Yields 4 cups

Marinated Cucumber

1 cucumber, skin left on
3 tablespoons cooking oil
2 teaspoons minced garlic
1 teaspoon sesame oil
$1^1/2$ teaspoons sugar
$1/2$ teaspoon salt

1 Wash the cucumber, quarter it lengthwise and discard the seeds. Cut the flesh into matchstick pieces and place them in a bowl.
2 Heat the cooking oil and stir-fry the garlic for a few seconds until it turns golden, then discard the garlic and pour the oil over the cucumber. Mix in the remaining ingredients and chill. Serve as a starter, or as an accompaniment to any Chinese dish.

Preparation time: 10 mins + chilling time
Yields 3 cups

Pickled Garlic

1 cup (250 ml) water
2 bulbs garlic cloves, skins left on
$1/2$ cup (125 ml) white vinegar
$1^1/2$ tablespoons sugar
$1/2$ teaspoon salt
1 small bay leaf

1 Bring the water to a boil in a large saucepan. Add the garlic and the remaining ingredients and set aside to cool.
2 Place the garlic in a dry, glass jar, top with the liquid and leave to marinate for 1 day before using. Drain and serve as an accompaniment or appetizer.

Preparation time: 5 mins + 1 day marinating time   Yields 2 pickled garlic bulbs

Spicy Cabbage Pickles

1 small Chinese cabbage
2 teaspoons salt
3 fresh red chilies, deseeded and cut
  into thin strips
1 in (2 cm) ginger, peeled and grated
4 tablespoons sugar
4 tablespoons white vinegar
1 tablespoon oil

1 Wash and dry the cabbage leaves. Slice the leaves into thin ribbons and place into a bowl. Sprinkle with the salt, mix, and set aside for 1 hour.
2 Drain the cabbage of any excess liquid, squeezing gently, and place it in a clean bowl. Add the remaining ingredients, except for the oil and mix well.
3 Heat the oil and pour it over the cabbage. Store in a dry, glass container in the refrigerator and marinate for 2 days before enjoying as a side dish.

Preparation time: 1 hour 10 mins + 2 days marinating time
Yields 4 cups

Sauces and Dips

Ginger Garlic Sauce

4 in (10 cm) ginger, peeled and
  sliced
6 cloves garlic
1 teaspoon salt
1 teaspoon sugar
1 teaspoon sesame oil
1 tablespoon cooking oil

1 Process the ginger and garlic in a food processor until fine. Combine with the remaining ingredients and store in a covered jar. Shake just before serving.

Chili Garlic Sauce

5 fresh red chilies
3 cloves garlic
3 tablespoons white vinegar
1 teaspoon sugar
$1/2$ teaspoon salt

1 Process all the ingredients in a food processor until smooth. Store refrigerated in a dry, covered jar. Serve with steamed poultry or rice.

Ginger and Soy Dip

2 tablespoons grated ginger
2 teaspoons soy sauce
1 tablespoon finely sliced spring onion
$1/2$ teaspoon sugar
2 tablespoons peanut oil
$1/2$ tablespoon sesame oil

1 Combine ginger, soy sauce, spring onion, and sugar. Heat both oils in a small saucepan together until they smoke, then pour over the ginger mixture and stir. Serve immediately with steamed chicken or fish.

Ginger Black Vinegar Dip

3 in (8 cm) ginger, peeled and cut into thin shreds
3 tablespoons black vinegar

1 Combine the ginger and vinegar together. Serve with dumplings and other *dim sum* dishes.

Sesame Sauce

4 tablespoons sesame seeds
4 tablespoons chicken stock or water
$1/2$ teaspoon sesame oil
$1/2$ teaspoon salt
$1/2$ teaspoon sugar

1 Heat a dry skillet gently over low heat and dry-roast the sesame seeds for 1 to 2 minutes.
2 Place the sesame seeds in a spice grinder or food processor with the chicken stock or water and grind to a paste. Mix in the remaining ingredients and serve with any seafood dish.

Hot Soy Dipping Sauce

3 tablespoons soy sauce
$2^1/2$ tablespoons white vinegar
1 tablespoon Worcestershire sauce
1 tablespoon ground Sichuan peppercorns or *sansho* pepper
1 tablespoon finely sliced spring onion
1 teaspoon sesame oil

1 Mix all the ingredients together in a bowl. This sauce is excellent as a marinade for meats, or as a dip for steamed vegetables. The use of the English Worcestershire sauce is unconventional and reflects the Chinese cook's willingness to adapt to anything that might improve the flavor of food.

Soup Stocks

Homemade Chicken Stock

3 lbs ($1^1/2$ kgs) chicken bones or $1/2$ chicken
2 in (5 cm) ginger, sliced
3 spring onions or shallots
1 celery stalk, leaves attached, roughly chopped
1 teaspoon peppercorns
10 cups ($2^1/2$ liters) water

1 Combine all the ingredients in a large stock pot and bring to a boil over high heat. Reduce the heat and simmer for 1 hour. Discard the solids and strain the stock through a fine sieve. The stock can be frozen for up to 3 months.

Yields 8 cups (2 liters)
Preparation time: 5 mins
Cooking time: 1 hour

Homemade Vegetable Stock

1 teaspoon oil
1 carrot, peeled
1 celery stalk, leaves attached, roughly chopped
2 in (5 cm) ginger, sliced
3 spring onions or shallots
3 garlic cloves
6 dried black mushrooms, soaked, stems discarded, and caps diced
$1/2$ teaspoon salt
$1/2$ teaspoon peppercorns
10 cups ($2^1/2$ liters) water

1 Heat the oil in a large stock pot over medium high heat. Add the carrot, celery, ginger, spring onions, garlic, and mushrooms and stir-fry for 3 to 4 minutes.
2 Add the remaining ingredients and increase the heat to high and bring to a boil. Reduce the heat and simmer for 1 hour. Strain the stock through a sieve and discard the solids.

Yields 8 cups (2 liters)
Preparation time: 5 mins
Cooking time: 1 hour

Pork Dumplings in Hot Sauce

Dumplings are a favorite snack in most of China, from Beijing in the north to Shanghai on the east coast, from the southern province of Guangdong to Sichuan in the far west. The fillings differ from one area to another, as well as according to season. In summer in Beijing, the basic pork stuffing might be seasoned with fresh dill or chopped Chinese chives. The dumplings may be steamed, fried, boiled, served in soup (like the famous Cantonese wonton soup), or, as in this Sichuan version, bathed in a tangy sauce.

Filling
8 oz (250 g) ground pork
1 egg, lightly beaten
$1^1/_2$ teaspoons grated ginger
2 tablespoons rice wine or sake
1 teaspoon salt
$^1/_4$ teaspoon ground white pepper
25 wonton wrappers

Sauce
1 clove garlic, minced
4 tablespoons soy sauce
1 tablespoon chili oil
$^1/_2$ teaspoon sugar
$^1/_2$ teaspoon ground cinnamon
2 spring onions, finely sliced

1 To make the Filling, combine all the ingredients, except for the wonton wrappers, and mix well.
2 Place a teaspoonful of the Filling in the center of a wonton wrapper and use a fingertip dipped in water to moisten the edge of the wonton wrapper. Fold the wrapper in half to make a semi-circle, then press firmly to enclose the Filling, making sure there are no air pockets inside the wonton. Repeat until all the Filling is used up.
3 Carefully lower the dumplings into a pot of boiling water with a strainer or slotted spoon. Simmer for 2 to 3 minutes and drain.
4 To prepare 4 servings, place $^1/_4$ teaspoon garlic, 1 tablespoon soy sauce, a $^1/_4$ teaspoon chili oil, a pinch of sugar, and a pinch of cinnamon in the bottom of 4 bowls. Divide the boiled dumplings among the bowls and garnish with sliced spring onion.

Makes 25 dumplings   Preparation time: 30 mins   Cooking time: 5 mins

Steamed Vegetable Dumplings with Black Vinegar Sauce

Tender parcels of stir-fried vegetables served with a hot and tangy sauce.

Filling
1 tablespoon oil
4 cloves garlic, minced
1 tablespoon grated ginger
6 dried black Chinese mushrooms,
   soaked in warm water for 10 minutes,
   stems discarded, and caps diced
1 teaspoon sesame oil
2 teaspoons soy sauce
2 cups (250 g) grated carrot
2 cups (250 g) shredded Chinese
   cabbage
$1/2$ cup (100 g) water chestnuts, diced
2 spring onions, finely sliced
40 round wonton wrappers, 4 in
   (10 cm) across

Black Vinegar Sauce
2 tablespoons soy sauce
2 tablespoons chili oil
4 tablespoons black vinegar
$1/2$ teaspoon sesame seeds
1 spring onion, thinly sliced

1 To make the Filling, heat the oil in a wok over medium heat. Add the garlic, ginger, mushrooms, sesame oil, and soy sauce, and stir-fry for 1 to 2 minutes. Add the carrot, cabbage, water chestnuts, and spring onion, stir-fry for 2 to 3 minutes until the vegetables soften, then remove from the heat. Place the vegetables in a bowl, draining any liquid before using.
2 Place a wonton wrapper on a clean, dry surface. Place $1/2$ tablespoon of vegetable filling in the center of a wrapper, gather the edges around the Filling to form a pouch, then press the edges of the wrapper firmly to seal. Set aside and repeat with the remaining wonton skins and Filling. Arrange all the wontons on a lightly-oiled plate and steam covered in a bamboo steamer for 10 minutes.
3 Prepare the Black Vinegar Sauce by combining the soy sauce, chili oil, and black vinegar in a small bowl, then sprinkle with sesame seeds and spring onion. Remove the wontons from the steamer and serve with the Black Vinegar Sauce.

Note: White Peking wonton wrappers, sold in some Asian markets, give these wontons a chewy texture and make a nice presentation.

Makes 40 wontons   Preparation time: 30 mins   Cooking time: 17 mins

Lettuce Cups with Mushrooms and Tofu

A quick, fresh appetizer that's fun to eat! The filling has a delicate crunchy texture and a touch of sweetness. These tasty cups can also be made with ground turkey or pork, in place of the tofu called for here.

6 dried black Chinese mushrooms soaked in warm water for 10 minutes, stems discarded, and caps diced
1 tablespoon oil
2 cloves garlic, minced
1 tablespoon grated ginger
1 tablespoon rice wine or sake
10 oz (320 g) firm tofu, cubed
1 teaspoon sesame oil
$1/4$ teaspoon freshly ground black pepper
1 carrot, peeled and diced
$1/2$ cup (90 g) diced water chestnuts
1 head Butter or Red Leaf lettuce, leaves washed and patted dry
Spring onions, sliced, to garnish
Sesame seeds, to garnish
Hoisin sauce, to serve
Chili Garlic Sauce (page 25), to serve

1 Drain the mushrooms, reserving $1/4$ cup (60 ml) of the soaking liquid.
2 Heat 1 tablespoon of oil in a wok, add the tofu and fry until light brown on all sides, about 5 minutes. Remove, drain on paper towels and set aside.
3 Heat the remaining oil in a wok over medium-high heat. Add the mushrooms, garlic, ginger, and rice wine, and stir-fry for 30 seconds. Add the sesame oil and black pepper, and stir-fry for 2 to 3 minutes, then add the reserved mushroom liquid and diced carrot, and stir-fry for 2 minutes. Stir in the water chestnuts and mix thoroughly.
4 Fill each lettuce leaf with 2 to 3 tablespoons of the filling, sprinkle with spring onion and sesame seeds, and serve with hoisin sauce and Chili Garlic Sauce (page 25).

Note: If using ground turkey or pork in place of the tofu, omit step 2 and stir-fry $1/2$ lb (250 g) fresh ground turkey or pork at the beginning of step 3 until the meat is browned, then continue with the remaining steps.

Serves 4–6   Preparation time: 30 mins   Cooking time: 7 mins

Classic Egg Rolls

An all-time favorite, these golden egg rolls are filled with crunchy vegetables and savory pork. Accompanied with fragrant Jasmine tea, they make the perfect snack.

3 teaspoons cornstarch
1 teaspoon soy sauce
8 oz (250 g) ground pork, or diced ham or bacon
2 tablespoons oil
$1/2$ cup (90 g) thinly slivered bamboo shoots
2 carrots, peeled and grated
2 cups (180 g) thinly sliced Chinese cabbage
2 spring onions, sliced
2 cups (100 g) fresh bean sprouts
1 teaspoon salt
$1/4$ teaspoon pepper
20 spring roll wrappers
1 egg, beaten
Oil for deep-frying
Plum sauce, to serve
Hot Chinese or English mustard, to serve

1 Blend 1 teaspoon of the cornstarch with the soy sauce and combine with the pork. Set aside.

2 Heat the oil in a wok over medium-high heat and stir-fry the pork until it changes color, about 3 minutes. Add the bamboo shoots and grated carrot and stir-fry for 2 minutes.

3 Add the cabbage and stir-fry for about 2 minutes, or until the cabbage is soft but still crisp. Remove from the heat and stir in the spring onions, bean sprouts, salt, and pepper. Drain the filling before using.

4 Lay a spring roll wrapper on a flat surface, with a corner facing you. Spoon 2 tablespoons of the filling onto the wrapper, about 2 in (5 cm) from the bottom corner. Shape the filling into a long, narrow strip.

5 Fold the bottom corner up and over the filling, and roll once, away from you. Dab a bit of egg on the left and right corners and fold each in, pressing to seal. Dab the top corner with a bit of egg and roll, sealing the egg roll. Repeat until all the wrappers and filling are used up.

6 Heat the oil in a wok over high heat until almost smoking. Add 5 egg rolls at a time and fry until crisp and golden, about 3 minutes. Remove the egg rolls with a slotted spoon and drain on paper towels. Serve with plum sauce, mustard, and a side of Spicy Cabbage Pickles (page 24).

Makes 20 egg rolls   Preparation time: 30 mins   Cooking time: 30 mins

Fold the bottom corner of the spring roll wrapper up and over the filling and roll once.

Dab a bit of beaten egg on the left and right corners, then fold them in, pressing to seal.

Dab a bit of beaten egg on the top corner and roll up to seal the egg roll. A spoon comes in handy for helping with this step, but your hands will work just fine.

Fresh Spring Rolls Bao Bing

A favorite in the southeastern province of Fujian, these tasty rolls are made with rice flour wrappers, which are available frozen or refrigerated in Asian food stores (*popiah* wrappers or *moo-shu* pancakes are good substitutes).

24 fresh or frozen rice flour wrappers
  (or *popiah* wrappers, or *moo shu*
  pancakes)
Chili paste

Filling
$1^1/_2$ tablespoons oil
8 oz (250 g) lean pork, cut into thin
  strips
3 cups (500 g) slivered bamboo
  shoots
10 oz (300 g) shrimp, peeled and
  deveined
1 large carrot, peeled and cut into
  matchsticks
5 cups (500 g) thinly sliced Chinese
  cabbage
1 cup (100 g) fresh bean sprouts or
  snow peas
7 cloves garlic, minced
$2^1/_2$ teaspoons salt
1 teaspoon sugar
$^1/_2$ teaspoon freshly ground black
  pepper
1 tablespoon rice wine or sake

Sweet Black Sauce
4 tablespoons brown sugar
1 cup (250 ml) water
3 tablespoons black soy sauce
1 tablespoon cornstarch
5 cloves garlic, minced

Accompaniments
Lettuce leaves, broken into small
  pieces
Fresh coriander leaves (cilantro),
  minced
Spring onions, sliced
Blended mustard or chili sauce, to
  serve

1 To make the Filling, heat the oil in a wok over high heat and stir-fry the pork and bamboo shoots for about 5 minutes, or until the pork changes color. Add the shrimp, carrot, cabbage, bean sprouts, and garlic, and stir-fry for 3 to 5 minutes, or until tender. Add the salt, sugar, pepper, and rice wine and mix well. Cover and cook for 3 more minutes, then set aside.

2 To make the Sweet Black Sauce, place the sugar and $^1/_4$ cup (60 ml) water in a saucepan over medium heat and swirl the contents gently to mix. Heat until the sauce is golden brown and the sugar has caramelized. In a small bowl, mix together the remaining water, soy sauce, and cornstarch, then add it to the saucepan. Simmer until the sauce thickens, then cool. Stir in the garlic and set aside.

3 Place a wrapper on a flat surface, then place a small piece of lettuce in the center of the wrapper (the lettuce will help absorb any liquid so the wrapper will not tear). Spread chili paste and Sweet Black Sauce to taste on the lettuce, then place 2 tablespoons of filling on top. Sprinkle with coriander leaves and spring onion, then roll up, tucking in the sides. Repeat with the remaining wrappers and Filling. Serve with blended mustard or chili sauce if desired.

Makes 24 spring rolls   Preparation time: 1 hour   Cooking time: 15 mins

Crispy Shrimp Toast

Shrimp toasts are typically served as triangular pieces of bread, spread with shrimp paste and deep-fried. This version includes whole shrimp in addition to the shrimp paste, and the bread can also be cut into disks with a cookie cutter, rather than triangles, to obtain the shape shown in the photo.

4 slices lightly toasted white bread
12 oz (350 g) shrimp, peeled and deveined
2 cloves garlic
1 tablespoon grated ginger
1 teaspoon sugar
$1/2$ teaspoon salt
1 egg white
$1/2$ teaspoon sesame oil
2 spring onions, sliced
1 egg, beaten
$1/2$ cup unseasoned breadcrumbs
Oil for deep-frying

Dipping Sauce
$1/4$ cup (60 g) sugar
$3/4$ cup (180 ml) rice vinegar
$1/4$ cup water
1 fresh red chili, deseeded and sliced
2 spring onions, very thinly sliced

1 To make the Dipping Sauce, combine the sugar, vinegar, and water in a small pan and stir over low heat until the sugar dissolves. Remove from the heat and stir in the chili and spring onion. Set aside.
2 Remove the crusts from the bread and cut each piece diagonally into 4 triangles, or use a cookie cutter to cut out circles.
3 Set aside 12 shrimp. Place the remaining shrimp, garlic, ginger, sugar, salt, egg white, and sesame oil into a food processor or blender and process until smooth. Stir in the spring onions.
4 Spread a tablespoon of the shrimp paste on each piece of bread and place a reserved shrimp on top. Brush the shrimp paste with beaten egg and sprinkle with breadcrumbs.
5 Heat the oil in a wok over medium-high heat. Fry the bread pieces a few at a time until crisp and golden, about 1 minute per side. Remove with a slotted spoon and drain on paper towels. Serve hot with the Dipping Sauce.

Makes 12–14   Preparation time: 5 mins   Cooking time: 10 mins

Shrimp and Crab Tofu Skin Rolls   Chao Lian Xia Xie Jiao

The pure, fresh taste of seafood wrapped in crispy tofu skin and accompanied by Chili Garlic Sauce.

3–4 sheets dried tofu skin
6 oz (180 g) shrimp, peeled and deveined
5 fresh or canned water chestuts (60 g), peeled and drained
4 sprigs fresh coriander leaves (cilantro)
3 cloves garlic
$\frac{1}{2}$ teaspoon salt
4 oz (125 g) crabmeat, fresh or canned
2 spring onions, sliced
Oil for deep-frying

1 Soak the tofu skin in hot water until pliable, about 3 minutes. Cut the skin into 10, 5 in (12 cm) square pieces and set aside.
2 Combine the shrimp, water chestnut, fresh coriander leaves, garlic, and salt in a food processor and pulse until blended. Stir in the crabmeat and sliced spring onion.
3 Spread 2 to 3 tablespoons of the filling across the center of a piece of tofu skin. Fold the skin over the filling, fold the sides in, then fold over to seal the filling in. Repeat until all the filling is used up.
4 Heat the oil in a wok over high heat. Fry the rolls, a few at a time, until crisp and golden, about 2 minutes per side. Drain on paper towels and repeat until all the rolls are fried. Serve immediately with Chili Garlic Sauce (page 25), and Ginger Black Vinegar Dip (page 25).

Makes 9–10 rolls   Preparation time: 25 min   Cooking time: 10 min

Yunnan Ham Pastries   Cong Shao Huo Cui Bing

Crisp, golden brown pastry wrapped around succulent Yunnan ham, a delicious snack at any time of the day. These may be either baked, pan-fried, or deep-fried.

8 oz (250 g) Yunnan ham, prosciutto, or other dark ham, in one piece
7 spring onions, finely sliced
2 teaspoons sugar
2 teaspoons sesame oil
Oil for pan-frying or deep-frying

Pastry
2 cups (500 g) flour
6 tablespoons oil
2 teaspoons sesame oil
$1\frac{1}{4}$ cups (310 ml) warm water

1 If using Yunnan ham (which is raw and air-dried), place the ham in a steamer and steam for 30 minutes (there is no need to steam cooked ham). Cool, then mince the ham finely. Combine the minced ham with the spring onion, sugar, and sesame oil, then set aside.
2 To make the Pastry, place the flour, oil, and sesame oil in a large bowl and mix to combine. Gradually add the water to form a pliable dough, then divide the dough in half.
3 Shape 1 portion of the dough into a ball and set aside. Lightly flour a clean surface and roll out the other portion of dough into a flat sheet that is $\frac{1}{4}$ in (5 mm) thick. Place the ball of dough that was set aside earlier, in the center of the rolled out dough, and wrap it around the ball of dough to form a larger ball. Roll out the large ball to a flat sheet that is $\frac{1}{4}$ in (5 mm) thick.
4 Cut the dough into squares of 3 in (8 cm). Place a tablespoon of the ham mixture into the center of each square, then fold it over to form a triangle. Press the edges together to seal firmly.
5 To pan-fry the pastries, heat enough oil to cover the bottom of a skillet over high heat and fry the pastries, a few at a time, turning once when lightly golden, about 3 minutes on each side. Remove and drain on paper towels.
6 To deep-fry the pastries, heat the oil in a wok until the oil is very hot, then deep-fry the pastries, a few at a time, for a few seconds, or until crisp and golden brown. Alternatively, you may bake the pastries in a 350°F (180°C) oven for 35 minutes.

Makes 26 pieces   Preparation time: 1 hour   Cooking time: 20 mins

Barbecued Pork Char Siew

Bursting with sweet and spicy flavor, this recipe is very easy to prepare and makes a tasty treat on its own or when used as a filling for Steamed Buns (page 79).

12 oz (375 g) boneless pork
3 tablespoons hoisin sauce
3 tablespoons soy sauce
1 tablespoon honey
2 cloves garlic, minced
$1/_4$ teaspoon five-spice powder

1 Slice the pork into 2 in (5 cm) wide strips and place in a shallow dish.
2 Combine the remaining ingredients and pour over the pork. Marinate in the refrigerator for at least 4 hours. Remove the pork and place in a foil-lined pan, reserving the marinade.
3 Bake the pork at 350°F (180°C) for 30 minutes, turning and basting with the reserved marinade every 10 minutes. Thinly slice and serve.

Serves 4   Preparation time: 5 mins + 4 hours marinating time   Cooking time: 30 mins

Drunken Chicken

This classic cold dish stimulates the appetite before the main course—a great way to use leftover chicken!

2 chicken breasts or $1/_2$ chicken
$1/_4$ teaspoon salt
$1/_4$ teaspoon freshly ground black pepper
$3/_4$ cup (180 ml) chicken stock
3 tablespoons rice wine or sake
2 tablespoons soy sauce
1 teaspoon sugar
1 tablespoon grated ginger
Pinch of ground white pepper
3 spring onions, sliced

1 Line a medium-sized bamboo steamer with damp paper towels and set in a wok or large pan filled about $1/_3$ full of water (water should not touch the bottom rack of the steamer). Heat the water over high heat.
2 Season the chicken with salt and pepper and place in the steamer. Steam for 30 to 40 minutes, or until cooked through. Remove from the steamer, remove the skin, slice into bite-sized pieces, and set aside.
3 Combine the stock, rice wine, soy sauce, sugar, ginger, and white pepper in a large glass jar or bowl. Add the chicken and marinate at least 4 hours. Serve chilled, garnished with spring onion, with small bowls of Sesame Sauce (page 25) and Ginger and Soy Dip (page 25).

Serves 4–6   Preparation time: 5 mins + 4 hours marinating time
Cooking time: 30–40 mins

Crispy Fried Tofu

Tender blocks of tofu in a light, crispy coating served with a hot and sweet sauce.

1 lb (450 g) firm tofu
$1/_2$ cup (80 g) flour
1 teaspoon salt
1 teaspoon freshly ground black pepper
2 eggs, lightly beaten
1 cup (70 g) unseasoned breadcrumbs
Oil for deep-frying
2 spring onions, sliced

Dipping Sauce
$1/_2$ cup (125 ml) water
1 cup (200 g) sugar
$1/_2$ cup (125 ml) rice vinegar
1 fresh red chili, deseeded and minced
3 cloves garlic, minced
2 tablespoons plum sauce or apricot jam

1 To make the Dipping Sauce, combine the water, sugar, and rice vinegar in a small pan. Bring to a boil, reduce heat to low and cook until thick, about 30 minutes. Stir in the remaining Sauce ingredients, remove from the heat, and leave to cool.
2 Drain the tofu and wrap in several layers of paper towels, applying light pressure to remove the excess liquid. Cut into 2 in (5 cm) cubes and set aside.
3 Mix the flour, salt, and pepper in a small bowl. Dredge the tofu pieces in the flour mixture, dip in the beaten egg, and coat with the breadcrumbs.
4 Heat the oil in a wok over medium-high heat and deep-fry several pieces of tofu at a time until golden brown, about 5 seconds per side. Remove from the oil with a slotted spoon and drain on paper towels. Repeat until all the tofu pieces are fried. Top the tofu with sliced spring onion and serve with the Dipping Sauce.

Serves 4   Preparation time: 10 mins   Cooking time: 30 mins

Hot and Sour Soup Hai Xian Suan La Tang

This tangy Sichuan favorite combines tofu and dried mushrooms, but you can modify it by adding cooked shrimp, chicken or pork. Chili oil makes a nice condiment for this soup, and a touch of black vinegar or balsamic vinegar may be added when serving for extra zing.

4 cups (1 liter) chicken or vegetable stock
1 teaspoon salt
1 teaspoon sugar
$1/2$ tablespoon grated ginger
$1/2$ cup (60 g) fresh or frozen green peas
1 large tomato, diced
8 oz (250 g) soft tofu, diced
4 large fresh shiitake mushrooms, diced; or 4 dried black Chinese mushrooms, soaked in warm water, stems discarded, and caps diced
2 dried wood ear mushrooms, soaked in water and thinly sliced (optional)
2 tablespoons soy sauce
2 tablespoons black vinegar
1 teaspoon sesame oil
$1/2$ teaspoon freshly ground black pepper
$1/2$ teaspoon ground Sichuan peppercorns or *sansho* pepper
2 eggs, beaten
2 tablespoons cornstarch blended with 2 tablespoons water
4 spring onions, sliced
Pinch of ground white pepper
Chili oil, to serve (optional)
Black vinegar, to serve (optional)

1 Bring the stock to a boil in a large pot. Add the salt, sugar, ginger, peas, tomato, tofu, and mushrooms. Return to a boil and simmer for 3 minutes.
2 Add the soy sauce, vinegar, sesame oil, black pepper, and Sichuan pepper, and stir. Slowly drizzle the beaten eggs into the soup and let sit for 1 minute. Do not stir.
3 Stir the cornstarch mixture, then pour it slowly into the simmering soup while stirring gently. Keep stirring until the soup thickens. Simmer for 1 more minute, then turn off the heat.
4 Serve hot, garnished with spring onions and white pepper. Add a few drops of chili oil and black vinegar, if desired.

Serves 4   Preparation time: 30 mins   Cooking time: 10 mins

Sweet Corn and Crab Chowder

A comforting homestyle soup that can be made with fresh or frozen corn kernels, or with canned cream-style corn for a thicker consistency.

1 tablespoon oil
1 tablespoon rice wine or sake
2 thin slices of ginger
4 cups (1 liter) vegetable or chicken stock
5 dried black Chinese mushrooms, soaked in water for 20 minutes, stems discarded, and caps diced; or 8 button mushrooms, diced
1 small carrot, peeled and diced
1 cup (250 g) fresh or frozen sweet corn kernels, or 1 can (12 oz/350 g) cream-style corn
2 tablespoons fresh or frozen green peas
$1/2$ cup (100 g) cooked crab meat, or minced chicken
3 tablespoons cornstarch blended with 3 tablespoons water
$1/4$ teaspoon freshly ground black pepper
1 teaspoon sesame oil

1 Heat the oil in a wok over medium-high heat, then add the rice wine and ginger, letting it sizzle before adding the stock. Bring to a boil.
2 Add the mushrooms and carrot, simmer for 5 minutes, then add the corn, peas, crab meat, and salt. Simmer for another 5 minutes.
3 Stir in the cornstarch mixture, stirring until the soup thickens. Season with pepper and sesame oil before serving.

Serves 4   Preparation time: 30 mins   Cooking time: 20 mins

Tofu and Spinach Soup

A pure and simple soup that goes well with any meal.

4 cups (1 liter) chicken or vegetable stock
$1/2$ cake (125 g) soft tofu, cubed
1 tablespoon soy sauce
4 oz (125 g) spinach, washed, tough stems discarded, and leaves coarsely chopped
$1/4$ teaspoon ground white pepper

1 Bring the stock to a boil in a pot. Add the tofu and soy sauce and simmer for 2 minutes.
2 Add the spinach, cook for 2 minutes, then season with pepper and serve.

Serves 4   Preparation time: 5 mins   Cooking time: 10 mins

Egg Drop Soup

A traditional favorite. Ribbons of cooked egg swirled in a savory stock topped with a handful of spring onions.

4 cups (1 liter) chicken stock
1 tablespoon grated ginger
1 tablespoon soy sauce
1 tablespoon cornstarch, blended with 2 tablespoons water
2 eggs, lightly beaten
Pinch of salt and white pepper
4 spring onions, sliced, to garnish

1 Bring the chicken stock, ginger, and soy sauce to a boil in a saucepan. Add the cornstarch mixture, reduce the heat and bring the soup to a simmer.
2 Slowly pour in the beaten eggs, stirring constantly in the same direction. Turn off the heat and season with salt and pepper. Garnish each bowl of soup with a small handful of spring onions.

Serves 4   Preparation time: 5 mins   Cooking time: 15 mins

Fragrant Beef Noodle Soup

Cinnamon and star anise give this broth a wonderfully aromatic undertone which perfumes the kitchen and warms the body.

2¹/₂ lbs (1¹/₄ kgs) beef short ribs or
  beef shank
7 cups (1³/₄ liters) water
¹/₃ cup (90 ml) soy sauce
¹/₄ cup (60 ml) rice wine or sake
1 tablespoon sugar
2 in (5 cm) ginger, peeled and sliced
5 spring onions
3 cloves garlic, crushed
1 cinnamon stick
2 star anise pods
8 oz (250 g) bok choy
6–8 large dried black Chinese mushrooms, soaked in water, stems
  discarded and caps sliced
8 oz (250 g) dried rice vermicelli,
  soaked in water for 15 minutes,
  then drained
Spring onions, thinly sliced, to garnish
Fresh coriander leaves (cilantro),
  to garnish
1 teaspoon sesame oil
Chili oil, to taste

1 In a large pot, combine the short ribs, water, soy sauce, rice wine, and sugar, and bring to a boil. Reduce to a simmer, skimming the froth from the surface of the soup. Add the ginger, spring onion, garlic, cinnamon, and star anise, and simmer covered for 1 hour, or until the meat is tender, skimming the froth at regular intervals.
2 While the broth is simmering, blanch the bok choy briefly in boiling water, then drain and set aside.
3 Remove the ribs and slice the meat, discarding the fat and bones. Set the meat aside. Strain the broth and return it to the pot. Skim the fat from the surface of the soup with a large spoon, then add the mushrooms and simmer covered for 10 minutes.
4 Place some rice vermicelli, meat and bok choy in individual soup bowls, then ladle in some hot soup and mushrooms. Garnish with spring onion and fresh coriander leaves, and sprinkle each bowl with a little sesame oil and chili oil, if using. Serve with a dish of Pickled Green Chili (page 24).

Serves 6   Preparation time: 20 mins   Cooking time: 1 hour 10 mins

Delicate White Fish Soup

Firm, fresh white fish and baby bok choy simmered in a fragrant broth—quick to prepare and delicious!

6 oz (180 g) white fish, thinly sliced
1 teaspoon cornstarch
$1/2$ tablespoon oil
2 teaspoons sesame oil
3 cloves garlic, minced
1 in ($2^1/_2$ cm) ginger, bruised
2 tablespoons rice wine or sake
4 cups (1 liter) chicken or vegetable
  stock
$1/2$ cup (50 g) sliced bok choy
$1/2$ tablespoon soy sauce
$1/2$ teaspoon salt
$1/2$ teaspoon freshly ground black
  pepper
2 spring onions, sliced

1 Rinse the fish and pat it dry with paper towels. Sprinkle the fish with the cornstarch and set aside.
2 Heat both the oils in a pot over high heat. Add the garlic and stir-fry for 30 seconds, then add the ginger and rice wine, and stir briskly. Pour in the stock and bring to a boil.
3 Add the bok choy, soy sauce, salt, and pepper to the pot and bring to a boil. Add the fish and simmer for 4 to 5 minutes. Serve hot and garnish with spring onions.

Serves 4   Preparation time: 5 mins   Cooking time: 15 mins

Chicken and Ginseng Soup

Medicinal herbs are often cooked with chicken to make a soup that is regarded as being important for its restorative value. This soup, with ginseng and boxthorn berries, is not only tasty, but is good for the kidneys, lungs, eyes, and general health.

1 whole chicken (about $2^1/_2$–3 lbs
  ($1^1/_4$–$1^1/_2$ kgs), quartered
6 cups ($1^1/_2$ liters) water
2 in (5 cm) ginger, sliced
4 cloves garlic, peeled
1 ginseng root, about $3/_4$ oz (25 g) or
  2 tablespoons sliced ginseng root
1 tablespoon boxthorn berries
  (optional)
Pinch of ground white pepper

1 Clean the chicken and remove the skin and fat.
2 Bring the water to a boil in a large stock pot. Add all the ingredients, except for the white pepper, and return to a boil. Simmer uncovered over low heat for about 30 minutes, skimming off any foam that rises to the surface. Simmer covered for another 30 minutes.
3 Serve piping hot with ground white pepper and soy sauce on the side.

Note: Fresh ginseng roots are available in Asian food markets and dried roots are usually available from Chinese apothecaries. The powdered or ground variety from pure ginseng tea bags is a good alternative.

Serves 4   Preparation time: 5 mins   Cooking time: 1 hour

Winter Melon Soup Dong Gua Tang

Winter melon looks like a small, green or brown watermelon, and is believed to be very yin—cleansing and cooling for the body and good for the skin. Be sure to use good fresh chicken stock as that, along with the delicate winter melon, is the predominant flavor of this soup.

2 lbs (1 kg) winter melon
4 cups (1 liter) chicken stock
1 in ($2^1/_2$ cm) ginger, peeled and sliced
4 oz (120 g) straw or button mushrooms
6 asparagus spears, cut into bite-sized pieces
$^1/_4$ cup (60 g) cooked crabmeat
$^1/_2$ cup (125 g) shredded cooked chicken
Pinch of white pepper
$^1/_4$ teaspoon salt
1 spring onion, thinly sliced
1 tablespoon minced fresh coriander leaves (cilantro)

1 Peel the winter melon and remove the seeds and fibers. Cut the flesh into small cubes and set aside.
2 Bring the stock to a boil in a pot, then add the winter melon, ginger, mushrooms, asparagus, crabmeat, and chicken, and return to a boil. Lower the heat and simmer for 10 minutes, covered.
3 Add the salt and white pepper, and garnish with spring onion and fresh coriander leaves.

Note: A whole, hollowed out winter melon makes an impressive presentation for this soup when decoratively carved.

Serves 4   Preparation time: 10 mins   Cooking time: 10 mins

Classic Fried Rice

This dish can be made with just about any meat and vegetable leftovers you have on hand. A sliced red chili or bits of bell pepper or asparagus add a wonderful zing. Serve with tangy pickles or Hunan Chili Relish.

4 cups (500 g) cooked rice, cooled to room temperature, or in the refrigerator
3 teaspoons oil
2 eggs, lightly beaten
8 fresh medium shrimp, peeled, deveined, and diced
1/2 cup (60 g) thinly sliced chicken or pork
2 dried Chinese sausages (60 g), thinly sliced on the diagonal
4 spring onions, thinly sliced
1 fresh red chili, deseeded and minced (optional)
1/2 cup (40 g) diced bell pepper or asparagus or green peas or sliced cabbage
1/4 teaspoon salt

1 Break up the rice grains with a fork, or with your hands, and set aside.
2 Heat 1 teaspoon of oil in a wok. Pour in the beaten eggs and cook until set. Break the omelet into small pieces with a spatula, then remove from the wok and set aside.
3 Heat the remaining oil over high heat in the wok and stir-fry the remaining ingredients, except for the rice and salt, for 2 minutes. Add the rice and salt and stir-fry for another 4 to 5 minutes, turning constantly to brown the rice. Add the fried egg and serve with Hunan Chili Relish (page 23).

Note: If you don't have Chinese sausages, any kind of sausage, ham or bacon can be substituted.

Serves 4–6   Preparation time: 5 mins   Cooking time: 5 mins

Vegetarian Fried Rice

Red beans or peas, and tofu make this dish nutritionally complete; salted black beans and chilies pack it full of flavor.

4 cups (500 g) cooked rice, cooled to room temperature, or in the refrigerator
2 tablespoons salted black beans or black bean chili paste
6 oz (180 g) extra firm or pressed tofu or dried tofu skin, cut into thin strips
2 teaspoons soy sauce
3 tablespoons oil
3 red and green chilies, deseeded and minced
3 cloves garlic, sliced
1 small onion, minced
6 asparagus spears, cut into 1 in (2 1/2 cm) pieces
2 tablespoons cooked red azuki beans or 1/2 cup (60 g) fresh or frozen green peas
1/2 cup (50 g) fresh bean sprouts
1/4 teaspoon salt
1/4 teaspoon ground white pepper
1/2 cup (40 g) diced bell pepper or thinly sliced cabbage or broccoli stems

1 Break up the rice grains with a fork or with your hands, and set aside. Soak the black beans in warm water for 10 minutes, drain, and set aside.
2 Place the tofu or tofu skin into a bowl, add the soy sauce and marinate for 5 minutes. Heat 2 tablespoons of the oil in a wok over high heat and stir-fry the tofu or tofu skin until brown, about 5 minutes. Remove from the wok and set aside.
3 Reduce the heat to medium-high and add the remaining oil to the wok. Stir-fry the chilies, bell pepper or cabbage, garlic, and onion for 1 minute, then add the asparagus, black beans, azuki beans or peas, and bean sprouts, and stir-fry for another minute. Add the rice and tofu and season with salt and pepper, mixing well. Serve with Hunan Chili Relish (page 23).

Serves 4–6   Preparation time: 5 mins   Cooking time: 7 mins

Stir-fried Rice Vermicelli

The flavor of this satisfying vegetarian dish is brightened with a squeeze of fresh lime juice and a dollop of chili sauce, or a side dish of Pickled Green Chili.

8 oz (250 g) dried rice vermicelli
3 long, narrow sticks of dried tofu skin
3 tablespoons oil
3 cloves garlic, minced
1 in (2 cm) ginger, thinly shredded
12 dried black Chinese mushrooms, soaked in 1 cup (250 ml) of hot water for 20 minutes, stems discarded, and caps sliced; liquid reserved
10 oz (300 g) cabbage, sliced into very thin ribbons
1 carrot, peeled and grated
2 tablespoons soy sauce
2 teaspoons sugar
1 teaspoon salt
1/2 teaspoon ground white pepper
2 tablespoons mushroom sauce
1 cup (125 g) fresh bean sprouts
3 spring onions, cut into lengths
1 teaspoon sesame oil
1 fresh red chili, sliced, to garnish
1 lime, cut into wedges, to garnish

1 Soften the vermicelli by soaking it in enough water to cover, then drain and set aside. Soften the dried tofu skin by rinsing in water, then slice it into thin strips.

2 Heat 1 tablespoon of the oil in a wok over medium-high heat, stir-fry the tofu skin for 5 minutes until crispy, then remove and set aside.

3 Heat 2 tablespoons of the oil in a wok and stir-fry the garlic and ginger for 30 seconds. Add the mushrooms and stir-fry for 1 minute. Add the cabbage and 1/2 cup (125 ml) of the reserved mushroom liquid, and continue to stir-fry until the cabbage is slightly softened.

4 Add the drained vermicelli, carrot, soy sauce, sugar, salt, pepper, mushroom sauce, and another 1/2 cup (125 ml) of the reserved mushroom liquid. Stir-fry for 5 minutes, then stir in half of the tofu skin, bean sprouts, spring onions and sesame oil, and mix well. Garnish with the remaining tofu skin and red chili, and serve with wedges of lime, bottled chili sauce, or a side dish of Pickled Green Chili (page 24).

Serves 4   Preparation time: 20 min   Cooking time: 20 mins

Longevity Noodles

Symbolizing long life, longevity noodles are often served on birthdays and at Chinese New Year celebrations. This quick version is characterized by its pure and simple flavors, and the crunch of snow peas.

10 dried black Chinese mushrooms, soaked in 1 cup (250 ml) of hot water for 20 minutes, stems discarded and caps sliced; liquid reserved
1 teaspoon sesame oil
4 tablespoons soy sauce
2 tablespoons oil
$1^1/_2$ teaspoons salt
1 teaspoon sugar
4 oz (125 g) snow peas, ends trimmed
4 oz (125 g) bamboo shoots, sliced lengthwise (optional)
1 tablespoon grated ginger
1 lb (500 g) fresh egg noodles
8 Chinese chives or spring onions, cut into lengths
Pickled Green Chili (page 24), to serve

1 Combine $^1/_4$ cup (60 ml) of the reserved mushroom liquid with the sesame oil and soy sauce and set aside.
2 Bring a pot of salted water to a boil over high heat and cook the noodles for 1 minute. Drain, rinse with cold water, and set aside.
3 Heat 1 tablespoon of oil in a wok over high heat and add the mushrooms, salt and sugar. Stir-fry for 2 minutes, then add the snow peas and bamboo shoots, if using, and continue to stir-fry for 1 minute. Remove from the wok and set aside.
4 Add another tablespoon of oil to the wok, stir-fry the ginger for 30 seconds, then add the noodles, reserved mushroom liquid, and the vegetables stir-fried earlier. Sprinkle with spring onions and serve with a small dish of Pickled Green Chili (page 24).

Serves 4   Preparation time: 20 mins   Cooking time: 8 mins

Stir-fried Noodles with Shrimp and Pork

Very fine, fresh wheat flour noodles, like angel hair pasta, are used for this dish, popular in the southern coastal province of Fujian. The shrimp stock accents this dish with the wonderful taste of the sea.

10 oz (300 g) small shrimp
1 cup (250 ml) water
1 lb (500 g) fresh wheat flour noodles or 10 oz (300 g) dried rice vermicelli or wheat noodles
2 tablespoons oil
4 shallots, thinly sliced
13 cloves garlic, minced
4 oz (125 g) ground pork
2 cups (500 g) slivered bamboo shoots
1 carrot, peeled and cut into matchsticks
4 dried black Chinese mushrooms, soaked in hot water for 20 minutes, stems discarded, and caps diced
$1/4$ cup (60 g) coarsely chopped Chinese chives
2 tablespoons rice wine or sake
Pinch of salt and freshly ground black pepper

1 Peel the shrimp. Place the heads and shells in a small saucepan with the water and bring to a boil. Reduce the heat and simmer for 10 minutes. Mash the shells, then strain and reserve the broth, discarding the shells.
2 Blanch the noodles in boiling water for 1 minute. Drain and set aside.
3 Heat the oil in a wok over medium-high heat. Add the shallots and fry until golden brown, about 3 to 4 minutes. Drain, remove the shallots from the wok and set aside. Reserve the oil in the wok.
4 Add the garlic to the wok and stir-fry for 30 seconds. Add the shrimp, pork, bamboo shoots, carrot, mushrooms and chives. Stir-fry until the pork and shrimp change color, about 3 to 4 minutes. Pour in $1/2$ cup (125 ml) of the reserved shrimp stock, then add the rice wine, salt, and pepper, and simmer uncovered for 5 minutes, stirring occasionally.
5 Add the blanched noodles and stir-fry for 3 minutes. Mix well and serve.

Serves 4–6   Preparation time: 45 mins   Cooking time: 20 mins

Chilled Summer Noodles

If you've always eaten noodles piping hot, this dish might seem a little surprising. However, chilled noodles are a popular summer dish in China as well as in neighboring Japan. This dish is quick and easy to prepare and makes a nice lunch.Try to get fresh wheat noodles for this dish—they are available in most supermarkets.

8 oz (250 g) dried or 14 oz (400 g) fresh wheat flour noodles
$^3/_4$ cup (75 g) fresh bean sprouts
Spring onions, sliced, to garnish

Sauce
$2^1/_2$ tablespoons grated ginger
5 large cloves of garlic, crushed
1 tablespoon sesame paste or peanut butter
$^1/_2$ tablespoon oil
3 tablespoons soy sauce
2 teaspoons sugar
2 teaspoons black vinegar
$^1/_2$ tablespoon sesame oil
1 teaspoon chili oil

1 To make the Sauce, combine the ingredients and mix well. Alternatively, you may serve all the ingredients in small sauces as shown and allow each person to mix their own sauce at the table.
2 Cook the noodles according to the package directions, then drain well. Combine the noodles with the Sauce and bean sprouts, tossing gently. Take care not to break the bean sprouts.
3 Garnish with spring onion and serve immediately, or chill and serve later.

Serves 4   Preparation time: 10 mins   Cooking time: 3 mins

Hot and Spicy Sichuan Noodles   Dan Dan Mian

It's hard to think of any time of day when noodles are not popular in China; they're eaten for breakfast, as a mid-morning snack, for lunch, as something to keep you going until dinner, and as a late-night restorative. This spicy Sichuan favorite is often sold at street-side stalls and by mobile vendors, known as hawkers.

$1/_2$ tablespoon Sichuan peppercorns or *sansho* pepper

$1^1/_2$ tablespoons peanut oil

1 teaspoon oil

8 oz (250 g) ground pork

2 cups (500 ml) chicken stock

$1/_2$ cup (125 g) preserved, salted radish, diced

4 tablespoons soy sauce

$1^1/_2$ tablespoons black vinegar

1 tablespoon minced garlic

2 teaspoons sesame oil

1 teaspoon chili oil

$1/_4$ teaspoon ground white pepper

1 lb (500 g) fresh wheat flour noodles or 8 oz (250g) dried flat wheat noodles

4 spring onions, finely sliced, to garnish

1 Heat a wok over low heat and dry-fry the Sichuan peppercorns or *sansho* pepper for 2 to 3 minutes until fragrant. Add the peanut oil and cook over low heat for 10 minutes to infuse it with the flavor of the peppercorns. Cool, then strain the oil, discarding the peppercorns. Set aside.

2 Heat the oil in a wok over high heat and stir-fry the pork for 2 to 3 minutes, or until cooked. Set aside.

3 Combine the Sichuan peppercorn oil, chicken stock, preserved radish, soy sauce, black vinegar, garlic, sesame oil, chili oil and white pepper in a saucepan. Keep warm over medium heat.

5 Bring a pot of water to a boil and cook the noodles. Fresh noodles will take about 2 minutes to cook, dried noodles about 4 minutes. Drain the noodles, divide among 4 large soup bowls and pour in the hot broth. Top with the pork and garnish with spring onion. Serve immediately.

Serves 4   Preparation time: 20 mins   Cooking time: 15 mins

Fragrant Sichuan Eggplant Yu Xiang Qiezi

This dish provides a wonderful aromatic blend of flavors. The traditional recipe uses ground pork, but you may substitute diced shiitake mushrooms for a vegetarian version.

10 oz (300 g) eggplant, cut into strips
2 teaspoons salt
$^1/_2$ cup (125 ml) oil
6 cloves garlic, minced
3 tablespoons grated ginger
$^1/_2$ cup (60 g) lean ground pork or
   diced shiitake mushroom caps
2 teaspoons Sichuan chili paste
1 teaspoon salted soybeans, mashed
Spring onions, sliced, to garnish
Fresh coriander leaves (cilantro),
   minced, to garnish

Sauce
2 teaspoons soy sauce
2 teaspoons rice wine or sake
1 teaspoon sesame oil
1 teaspoon black vinegar
1 tablespoon sugar
$^1/_2$ teaspoon freshly ground black
   pepper
2 tablespoons water

1 To make the Sauce, combine the ingredients, then set aside.
2 Sprinkle the eggplant with the salt and let it sit for 10 minutes. Drain away any liquid, then rub off any remaining salt from the eggplant. Squeeze the eggplant to extract any additional liquid.
3 Heat the oil in a wok over high heat until the oil is very hot, then stir-fry the eggplant for 3 to 4 minutes. Turn off the heat, remove the eggplant from the wok and drain on a plate lined with paper towels. Set aside.
4 Discard all but 1 tablespoon of the oil, and stir-fry the garlic and ginger over high heat for 1 minute until fragrant. Add the pork and continue to stir-fry for 2 minutes. Add the chili paste and salted soybeans and continue to stir-fry.
5 Stir in the Sauce, then add the eggplant and stir-fry until everything is evenly coated with the Sauce. Cover and simmer for 3 to 4 minutes, or until heated through. Garnish with the spring onion and fresh coriander leaves.

Note: Once the oil in the wok is hot, drop in a piece of eggplant. If it sizzles and moves around, the oil is hot enough to start cooking. If not, wait a few minutes—the oil must be very hot or the eggplant will turn out greasy.

Serves 4   Preparation time: 25 mins   Cooking time: 10 mins

Stir-fried Vegetables

Whatever vegetables you have on hand can be substituted for this quick and easy stir-fry, which makes a wonderful side to any main dish.

2 teaspoons oil
3 oz (80 g) snow peas, ends trimmed
Pinch of salt
$^1/_2$ teaspoon sugar
8 dried black Chinese mushrooms,
   soaked in $^1/_2$ cup (125 ml) hot water
   for 15 minutes, stems discarded
   and caps sliced; liquid reserved
4 oz (125 g) bamboo shoots, sliced
$^1/_2$ tablespoon grated ginger
2 tablespoons rice wine or sake
$^1/_2$ teaspoon mushroom oyster sauce
$^1/_2$ teaspoon sesame oil
$^1/_4$ teaspoon soy sauce
Pinch of ground white pepper

1 Heat the oil in a wok over medium-high heat and stir-fry the snow peas with the salt and sugar for 30 seconds. Add the mushrooms, bamboo shoots, $^1/_4$ cup (60 ml) of the reserved mushroom liquid, and the remaining ingredients. Simmer for 2 minutes, then serve.

Serves 4   Preparation time: 20 mins   Cooking time: 5 mins

CLOCKWISE FROM TOP: Fragrant Sichuan Eggplant, Stir-fried Vegetables, and Quick Asparagus (recipe on page 66).

Stir-fried Chinese Broccoli with Beef

Bite-sized pieces of Chinese broccoli and succulent beef, stir-fried in a delicious mushroom oyster sauce.

8 oz (250 g) beef, thinly sliced
1 tablespoon oil
$1/2$ in (1 cm) ginger, thinly sliced
1 tablespoon minced garlic
12 oz (350 g) Chinese broccoli
(*kailan*), cut into bite-sized pieces,
stems separated from the leaves
$1/2$ tablespoon mushroom oyster
sauce

Marinade
3 teaspoons soy sauce
2 teaspoons mushroom oyster sauce
$1/2$ teaspoon freshly ground black
pepper
1 teaspoon sugar
2 teaspoons rice wine or sake
1 teaspoon cornstarch

1 Mix all the Marinade ingredients together and combine with the beef. Marinate for 30 minutes, or overnight.
2 Heat $1/2$ tablespoon of the oil in a wok over high heat and stir-fry the ginger for 30 seconds, then discard the ginger. Add the beef to the wok and stir-fry for about 1 minute until the beef changes color, then remove the beef from the wok and set aside.
3 Add the remaining oil to the wok, stir-fry the garlic for 30 seconds over high heat, then add the broccoli stems and stir-fry for 1 minute. Add the broccoli leaves to the wok and continue to stir-fry.
4 Stir in the mushroom oyster sauce and continue to cook for 1 minute, then return the beef to the wok, stir, heat through, and serve.

Serves 4   Preparation time: 10 mins + 30 mins marinating time
Cooking time: 10 mins

Hoisin-glazed Green Beans

Tender-crisp green beans bathed in a sweet and spicy sauce—an irresistable combination!

1 tablespoon oil
1 tablespoon minced garlic
12 oz (350 g) green beans, ends trimmed, halved
3 tablespoons hoisin sauce
1¹/₂ tablespoons soy sauce
1 teaspoon sesame oil
2 teaspoons Chili Garlic Sauce (page 25), or 1 fresh red chili, minced

1 Heat the oil in a wok over high heat until smoking. Add the garlic, stir-fry for 1 minute, then gently slide the beans into the wok and stir-fry for 2 minutes.
2 Stir in the hoisin sauce, soy sauce, sesame oil, and Chili Garlic Sauce. Continue to stir-fry for 1 to 2 minutes until the beans are cooked and tender-crisp.

Note: This recipe is excellent with long beans or French green beans, if you can find them. Leave the beans to cook covered over medium heat for an additional 2 to 3 minutes if you prefer a softer texture.

Serves 4   Preparation time: 5 mins   Cooking time: 7 mins

Crunchy and Tangy Fresh Lotus Root Salad   Ma La Lian Ou

The lotus has special association for Buddhists for it is said that Gautama Buddha likened man striving to achieve goodness to an exquisite lotus bloom rising unsullied from the muddy bottom of a lake. This pure, refreshing dish is certain to lead you to enlightenment.

2 fresh lotus roots, about 8 oz (225 g)
1 tablespoon oil
2 spring onions, sliced
$1/_2$ teaspoon salt
1 teaspoon sugar
$1/_2$ cup (125 ml) water
1 tablespoon rice vinegar

1 Wash the lotus roots thoroughly, then peel and slice them crosswise into thin round pieces.
2 Heat the oil in a wok over high heat and stir-fry the lotus root, spring onion, salt, and $1/_2$ a teaspoon of sugar for 3 minutes.
3 Add the water, cover, then reduce the heat to medium and allow the lotus root to steam for 5 minutes. Remove the lotus root pieces from the wok with a slotted spoon and transfer them to a serving dish. Drizzle with some rice vinegar, sprinkle with the remaining sugar, and serve.

Note: It is best to purchase fresh lotus roots in an Asian food store for this dish, as canned roots do not have the same flavor and texture. Jicama (*bang kuang*) is a good substitute if lotus root is unavailable.

Serves 4   Preparation time: 5 mins   Cooking time: 8 mins

Hot and Sour Chinese Cabbage

Tender-crisp Chinese cabbage, stir-fried with shrimp, and seasoned in a hot and tangy sauce.

1 small Chinese cabbage (1 lb/500 g)
1 tablespoon oil
1 fresh red chili, minced
1 tablespoon minced ginger
1 cup (150 g) small shrimp or $^1/_4$ cup (60 g) dried shrimp
1 teaspoon sesame oil

Sauce
2 tablespoons soy sauce
$^1/_2$ teaspoon salt
2 tablespoons sugar
2 tablespoons black vinegar
1 tablespoon rice wine or sake

1 To prepare the Sauce, combine the ingredients in a bowl, then set aside.
2 Wash the cabbage leaves, discarding any wilted outer leaves, then drain thoroughly. Halve each leaf lengthwise, then quarter the halved leaves. Separate the harder stems from the softer leaves and set aside. If using dried shrimp, soak them first in hot water for 15 minutes to soften them. Drain, then chop them into smaller bits (a food processor is a quick and easy way to chop the dried shrimp).
3 Heat the oil in a wok over high heat until very hot and stir-fry the chili and ginger for 15 seconds. Add the shrimp and stir-fry for another 15 seconds.
4 Place the cabbage stems in the wok first, stir-fry for 1 to 2 minutes, then add the leaves and stir-fry for 1 minute. Sprinkle with the sesame oil, mix thoroughly, and serve with rice.

Serves 4–6   Preparation time: 15 mins   Cooking time: 10 mins

Tofu-stuffed Vegetables

This Cantonese and Hakka favorite is usually stuffed with a shrimp filling. This vegetarian version uses tofu and mushrooms instead of shrimp for the filling and is excellent with black bean sauce, which gives an emphatic salty tang to the delicate stuffed vegetables.

4 small green or red bell peppers
1 long Asian eggplant or bitter gourd
Oil for deep-frying

Stuffing
8 oz (250 g) firm tofu, drained
1 clove garlic, minced
3 fresh shiitake mushrooms or 2 dried
  black Chinese mushrooms, soaked
  in hot water for 10 minutes, stems
  discarded, and caps diced
$1/4$ teaspoon salt
$1/4$ teaspoon ground white pepper
1 egg, lightly beaten
1 spring onion, sliced

Sauce
1 tablespoon salted black beans,
  soaked and slightly mashed
1 fresh red chili, deseeded and
  minced
1 clove garlic, minced
1 tablespoon grated ginger
1 cup (250 ml) chicken or vegetable
  stock
1 teaspoon soy sauce
2 teaspoons cornstarch, blended
  with 2 teaspoons water

1 To make the Stuffing, mash the tofu then combine it with the remaining ingredients. Set aside.
2 Halve the bell peppers crosswise, and discard the white membrane and the seeds. Cut the eggplant into short sections of equal length. Make a deep slit down the side of each short section of eggplant, to form a pocket for the stuffing. Gently stuff the vegetables.
3 Steam the eggplant and bell peppers for 10 minutes, then drain away any excess liquid. Pat the eggplant and bell peppers dry with paper towels.
4 Heat the oil in a wok over high heat and gently deep-fry the eggplant and bell peppers in batches, stuffing side down, for 3 minutes. Turn the eggplant and bell peppers stuffing side up, and deep-fry for another 3 minutes. Drain, discard the oil, and return the wok to the stove.
5 To make the Sauce, add the black beans, chili, garlic and ginger to the wok and stir-fry for 30 seconds. Add the remaining ingredients and stir until thickened. Lower the heat to medium-low, add the eggplant and bell peppers, and simmer for 3 minutes. Serve hot.

Note: Be sure to use a splatter screen when frying as the high water content in the vegetables may cause the oil to pop and spatter.

Serves 2–4   Preparation time: 10 mins   Cooking time: 20 mins

Quick Asparagus

Fresh asparagus spears braised in a delicate broth and topped with salty slivers of ham (photo on page 61)—a feast for the senses!

1 cup (250 ml) water
$1/4$ teaspoon salt
$1/4$ teaspoon sugar
8 oz (250 g) young asparagus spears
$3/4$ cup (180 ml) chicken stock
1 teaspoon rice wine or sake
1 teaspoon soy sauce
$1/4$ teaspoon sesame oil
1 tablespoon slivered Yunnan or salted Parma ham, to garnish (optional)

1 Bring the water, salt, and sugar to a boil in a wok, and blanch the asparagus for 2 minutes. Drain the water and add the stock, wine, soy sauce, and sesame oil. Bring to a boil and simmer for 1 minute.
2 Serve hot, garnished with slivers of ham.

Serves 2   Preparation time: 2 mins   Cooking time: 3 mins

Ma Po Tofu

This is a classic Sichuan dish. Ground beef or dried shrimp may be substituted for the pork in this dish, however the dominant ingredient is tofu laced with pungent Sichuan seasonings. A vegetarian version can be made where the meat is omitted altogether, and substituted with fresh shiitake or dried black Chinese mushrooms.

2 tablespoons salted black beans
1 lb (500 g) firm tofu
2 tablespoons oil
6 oz (170 g) ground pork
1 tablespoon grated ginger
4 tablespoons minced spicy Sichuan pickles (*zha cai*—optional)
2 cloves garlic, minced
2 tablespoons chili paste
4 spring onions, thinly sliced
$^{1}/_{2}$ cup (125 ml) chicken stock
1 tablespoon soy sauce
2 teaspoons cornstarch, blended with 2 teaspoons water
$^{1}/_{2}$ teaspoon ground Sichuan peppercorns or *sansho* pepper

1 Cover the black beans with water and leave to soak for 10 minutes. Drain, then mash slightly with a fork and set aside.
2 Drain the tofu, place it between 2 plates, and top with a weight for 10 minutes. Drain any additional liquid, then dice the tofu and set it aside.
3 Heat the oil in a wok over medium-high heat and stir-fry the black beans and pork until the meat is completely browned, about 3 minutes. Add the ginger, Sichuan pickles (if using), garlic, chili paste, and half of the spring onions. Stir-fry for another 2 minutes, then add the chicken stock and tofu. Simmer for 5 minutes.
4 Add the soy sauce, then pour in the cornstarch mixture and stir until the sauce thickens. Sprinkle with Sichuan pepper and spring onion.

Note: For a vegetarian version, substitute 6 fresh shiitake or 8 dried black Chinese mushrooms. If using fresh mushrooms, discard the stems and dice the caps. If using dried black Chinese mushrooms, soak them in warm water for 15 minutes to soften, then drain, discard the stems, and dice the caps. Add the mushrooms in step 3 in place of the meat. The vegetarian version is much more flavorful if spicy Sichuan pickles (*zha cai*) are added.

Serves 4   Preparation time: 20 mins   Cooking time: 10 mins

Black Bean Chicken

Tender chicken and crisp snow peas simmered in a flavorful, salty black bean sauce.

2 skinless chicken breast fillets (1 lb/
  450 g), cut into strips
1/2 tablespoon grated ginger
1/2 tablespoon cornstarch, blended
  with 1 tablespoon rice wine or sake
2 tablespoons oil
4 shallots, diced
1 clove garlic, minced
2 tablespoons black bean and garlic
  sauce, or 1/3 cup (20 g) salted
  black beans, soaked and mashed
1/2 cup (125 ml) chicken stock
11/2 teaspoons sugar
1 cup (80 g) snow peas (optional)

1 Combine the chicken strips with the ginger and cornstarch mixture, and leave to marinate for 10 minutes.
2 Heat the oil in a wok over medium-high heat. When the oil is hot, add the shallots and garlic, and stir-fry for 30 seconds. Add the black bean and garlic sauce (or Chinese black beans) and stir-fry for another 30 seconds.
3 Add the chicken, chicken stock, and sugar and bring to a boil. Reduce the heat to low and simmer for 3 minutes. Add the snow peas, if using, and cook for another 2 minutes, or until the snow peas have softened.

Note: If using whole salted black beans, soak the beans in enough hot water to cover for 30 minutes. Rinse, drain, then roughly mash the beans.

Serves 4   Preparation time: 20 mins + 10 mins marinating time
Cooking time: 10 mins

Hunan Chicken Salad

Like its Sichuan cousin, Hunan cuisine makes liberal use of chili peppers. The hot and sweet sauce that dresses this salad contrasts beautifully with the steamed chicken and cool, crisp vegetables.

2 chicken breast fillets (1 lb/450 g)
1 small carrot, peeled and grated
1 small cucumber, cut into thin shreds
2 spring onions, sliced
2 tablespoons unsalted, roasted
 peanuts, coarsely chopped
Fresh coriander leaves (cilantro),
 minced, to garnish

Marinade
2 tablespoons grated ginger
2 tablespoons rice wine or sake
1 teaspoon sugar
$1/2$ teaspoon salt

Sauce
$1/4$ cup (60 ml) chicken stock
2 tablespoons soy sauce
$1^1/2$ tablespoon black vinegar
1 teaspoon sesame oil
2 teaspoons sugar
$1/2$ teaspoon Chili Garlic Sauce (p 25)

1 Mix all the Marinade ingredients together, combine with the chicken breasts and set aside for 30 minutes.

2 In the meantime, combine the Sauce ingredients and bring to a boil in a small saucepan. Remove from the heat and set aside.

3 When the chicken is finished marinating, drain, then place on a plate in a steamer and steam for 8 to 10 minutes. Remove the chicken and shred it into thin strips.

4 Arrange the carrot and cucumber on a platter and top with the shredded chicken, spring onion, and peanuts. Spoon the Sauce over the salad and garnish with the minced fresh coriander leaves.

Serves 2–4   Preparation time: 20 mins + 30 mins marinating time
Cooking time: 10 mins

Fried Chicken in a Tangy Hot Sauce

Crisp, yet tender morsels of chicken stir-fried with a sweet-sour chili sauce, perfect with steamed broccoli.

12 oz (350 g) boneless, skinless
  chicken, cut into bite-sized pieces
Pinch of salt and pepper
$^1/_4$ cup (60 g) cornstarch, blended
  with $^1/_2$ cup (125 ml) water
Oil for deep-frying
1 tablespoon oil
2 fresh red chilies, deseeded and
  minced
2 cloves garlic, minced
2 teaspoons grated ginger
$^1/_4$ cup (60 ml) chicken stock
1 tablespoon black vinegar
1 tablespoon sugar
$^1/_2$ tablespoon soy sauce
$^1/_4$ cup (60 ml) rice wine or sake
2 teaspoons cornstarch, blended
  with 2 teaspoons of water
Fresh coriander leaves (cilantro),
  coarsely chopped, to garnish

1 Season the chicken pieces by combining with the salt and pepper. In a small bowl, blend the cornstarch mixture with 2 teaspoons of oil. Coat the chicken pieces with the cornstarch mixture.

2 Heat the oil in a wok and deep-fry the chicken over high heat until crisp and golden. Drain on paper towels, then set the chicken aside. Discard the oil.

3 Heat 1 tablespoon of fresh oil in the wok and stir-fry the chilies for 30 seconds. Add the garlic and ginger, stir-fry for 30 seconds, then add the remaining ingredients, except for the cornstarch mixture and the coriander leaves. Stir to heat through.

4 Add the cornstarch mixture and continue to stir until the sauce thickens, then add the chicken pieces, coating thoroughly. Garnish with fresh coriander leaves and serve with a bowl of steamed broccoli.

Note: The first step in the recipe is a technique called "velveting"—coating the chicken with a bit of oil prevents it from drying up during deep-frying, while the cornstarch acts as a natural tenderizer.

Serves 4   Preparation time: 10 mins   Cooking time: 20 mins

Braised Chicken Wings in Plum Orange Sauce

Chinese chicken wings are usually deep-fried and then braised in sauce—this recipe is an easier, healthier version of this favorite dish.

2$^1/_2$ lbs (1$^1/_4$ kgs) chicken wings
1 tablespoon soy sauce
1 teaspoon salt
2 tablespoons rice wine or sake
2 tablespoons grated ginger
2 tablespoons hoisin sauce
1 tablespoon cornstarch
Fresh spring onions, sliced, to garnish

Plum Orange Sauce
$^1/_2$ cup (125 ml) plum sauce
$^1/_2$ cup (125 ml) orange tangerine
 juice

1 To make the Plum Orange Sauce, combine the ingredients and set aside.
2 Combine the chicken wings with all the other ingredients, except for the spring onions, and marinate for 30 minutes.
3 Preheat the oven to 400°F (200°C). Place the chicken wings in the oven for 15 minutes. Remove from the oven and pat with paper towels to remove the excess oil.
4 Pour the Plum Orange Sauce over the wings, using tongs to turn and coat thoroughly. Return the wings to the oven and bake for another 15 minutes, or until cooked. Garnish with spring onions and serve.

Note: 1 cup (250 ml) of unsweetened pineapple juice may be substituted for Plum Orange Sauce for a lighter version of this recipe.

Serves 4   Preparation time: 10 mins + 30 mins marinating time
Cooking time: 45 mins

Kung Bao Chicken with Dried Chilies

Dried chilies, Sichuan peppercorns, and garlic give this popular dish a triple punch of intense flavor and spice.

2 tablespoons oil
6 dried chilies, deseeded and cut into $1/2$ in (1 cm) pieces
10 Sichuan peppercorns
1 in ($2^1/_2$ cm) ginger, thinly sliced
6-10 cloves garlic, peeled
1 lb (450 g) boneless, skinless chicken breast, cut into bite-sized pieces
4 spring onions, sliced into short lengths
$1/_4$ cup (30 g) dry-roasted, unsalted peanuts (optional)
Spring onion, sliced, to garnish

Sauce
$2/_3$ cup (150 ml) chicken stock
2 tablespoons soy sauce
2 tablespoons rice wine or sake
$3/_4$ teaspoon black vinegar
2 teaspoons sesame oil
2 teaspoons sugar
$1^1/_2$ teaspoons cornstarch

1 Make the Sauce by combining the chicken stock, soy sauce, rice wine, black vinegar, sesame oil, sugar, and cornstarch in a small bowl. Set aside.
2 Heat the oil in a wok over high heat until very hot. Add the dried chilies and stir-fry for 30 seconds, or until they are almost black and start to smoke. Remove the chilies and set aside. Add the Sichuan peppercorns and garlic cloves to the wok and stir-fry for 1 minute. Add the ginger and stir-fry for another 30 seconds. Add the chicken to the wok and stir-fry for 3 to 4 minutes, or until it completely changes color.
3 Add the spring onion and the Sauce. Mix well. Reduce the heat and simmer for 2 minutes, stirring continuously. Stir in the peanuts, if using, and garnish with spring onion.

Note: Turn on the exhaust fan in your kitchen, or open a window before scorching the chilies as this step releases a pungent smoke.

Serves 4   Preparation time: 10 mins   Cooking time: 10 mins

Sweet and Sour Shandong Chicken

This dish from the northeastern province of Shandong features a sweet, garlicky sauce with a subtle hot and sour flavor.

1 tablespoon oil
4 cloves garlic, minced
2 lbs (1 kg) boneless, skinless chicken breast, cut into bite-sized pieces
1 spring onion, white part only, slivered

Sauce
1 fresh red chili, deseeded and sliced
4 cloves garlic, sliced
1 teaspoon chili paste
1 cup (250 ml) chicken stock
1 tablespoon soy sauce
$1/_4$ cup (60 ml) rice vinegar
3 tablespoons sugar or honey

1 Combine the Sauce ingredients in a saucepan and bring to a boil slowly over medium-high heat. Simmer for 2 minutes, turn off the heat and set aside.
2 Heat the oil in a wok over medium-high heat. Add the garlic and stir-fry until brown and crisp, about 3 to 4 minutes. Remove the garlic from the wok and set aside. Increase the heat to high, add half the chicken and stir-fry for about 5 minutes, or until browned and cooked through. Remove from the wok and drain on paper towels, then repeat with the remaining chicken.
3 Return all the chicken to the wok, add the Sauce and mix well. Serve on a platter garnished with the crispy fried garlic and slivered spring onion.

Note: The photo at right shows a more elaborate version of this dish. To prepare this version, use 1 large, whole chicken (3 lbs/1$1/_2$ kgs). Bring a large pot of water to a boil and poach the chicken for 30 minutes. Drain and dry thoroughly. Deep-fry the whole chicken for 5 minutes on each side, then remove from oil and drain. Cut the chicken into bite-sized pieces and arrange on a serving platter. Pour the Sauce over the chicken and serve.

Serves 4   Preparation time: 5 mins   Cooking time: 17 mins

Tea-smoked Duck

Peking Duck is one of the most famous Chinese duck preparations, although many connoisseurs prefer the Sichuan style of smoking duck. Morsels of smoked duck meat and spring onions are tucked into steamed buns (*man tou*), smeared with a tangy sauce and served with a Sichuan peppercorn dip.

1 duck (6 lbs/3 kgs)
1 tablespoon salt
1 teaspoon ground Sichuan peppercorns or *sansho* pepper
3 spring onions
3 in (8 cm) ginger, sliced
$^1/_2$ cup (125 ml) rice wine or sake
$^3/_4$ cup (60 g) tea leaves
4 bay leaves
4 star anise pods
3 cinnamon sticks
Oil for deep-frying
Spring onions, sliced, to garnish

Sauce
$^1/_2$ cup (125 ml) hoisin sauce
$^1/_2$ teaspoon ground Sichuan peppercorns or *sansho* pepper
1 teaspoon sesame oil
1 teaspoon oil

Sichuan Peppper and Salt Dip
2 teaspoons ground Sichuan peppercorns or *sansho* pepper
1 teaspoon salt
$^1/_2$ teaspoon sugar

1 Combine the Sauce ingredients and place in a wide, shallow saucer.
2 Combine the Sichuan Pepper and Salt Dip ingredients in a small bowl and set aside.
3 Wash the duck thoroughly and pat it dry. Rub the duck inside and out with the salt and ground Sichuan pepper. Place the spring onions and the ginger inside the cavity and place the duck on a heatproof plate. Pour the rice wine over the duck and steam for 1 hour and 15 minutes in a large steamer. Remove from the steamer, then drain and set aside.
4 Place the tea leaves, bay leaves, star anise and cinnamon in a dry wok over high heat. Once the leaves start to smoke, reduce the heat to medium, and place a rack over the smoking ingredients. Place the duck on the rack, cover with a tight-fitting lid, and leave to smoke for 10 minutes.
5 Preheat the oven to 350°F (180°C). Place the duck in a roasting pan and roast for 1 hour.
6 Heat the oil in a wok over high heat. Add the duck and deep-fry for 10 minutes, turning the duck over after 5 minutes. Drain and cut into serving pieces. Garnish with spring onion and serve with the Sauce, Steamed Buns (recipe below), and Sichuan Pepper and Salt Dip.

Note: To minimize smoke in the kitchen, be sure to run your exhaust fan, and do not remove the lid from the wok until the smoking of the duck has been completed.

Serves 4   Preparation time: 20 mins   Cooking time: 2 hours 35 mins

Steamed Buns   Man Tou

$1^1/_2$ teaspoons active dry yeast
$^1/_2$ cup (125 ml) warm water
$^1/_4$ cup (50 g) superfine (caster)
   sugar
2 cups (250 g) all-purpose flour, sifted
3 teaspoons oil

1 Combine the yeast with 2 tablespoons of warm water, 1 teaspoon of sugar, and 1 teaspoon of flour in a small bowl. Mix and stand in a warm place until frothy, about 15 minutes.
2 Combine the remaining flour and sugar in a large bowl. Add the yeast mixture, remaining warm water, and 2 teaspoons of oil. Mix well and knead for 3 minutes. Place in an oiled bowl and stand in a warm place for 1 hour.
3 Punch down the dough and knead on a floured board until smooth, about 5 minutes. Pinch off lumps of dough about the size of a golf ball and roll out to circles of about 3 in ($7^1/_2$ cm) in diameter.
4 Brush the center of each circle with a touch of oil, fold the circle in half, then in half again to form a quarter-circle. Use the tines of a fork to slash the curved edge of the dough, so that the dumpling will resemble a flower after steaming.
5 Place the buns in a bamboo steamer lined with damp paper towels and steam for 5 minutes.

Makes 16   Preparation time: 1 hour 30 mins   Cooking time: 5 mins

Beggar's Chicken

According to legend, this dish was created by a poor man who stole a chicken. He was about to cook it on a fire when the landowner passed by. To conceal it, he hastily wrapped the chicken in mud and tossed it on the fire. Later, when the landowner had passed, he broke open the mud casing to find a succulent bird cooked inside. This more refined version features a savory stuffing and encases the chicken in dough.

1 large chicken, about 3 lbs (1$^1/_2$ kgs)
2 dried lotus leaves (optional)
2 tablespoons oil

Stuffing
5 oz (150 g) pork, finely shredded
3$^1/_2$ oz (100 g) salted mustard cabbage (*mei cai*)
5 dried black Chinese mushrooms, soaked and diced
3 tablespoons grated ginger
2 spring onions, sliced
1 teaspoon sugar
2 teaspoons soy sauce
2 tablespoons rice wine or sake

Dough
5 cups (1 kg) flour
2 cups (500 ml) warm water

1 Preheat the oven to 350°F (180°C).
2 Combine the Stuffing ingredients in a bowl and set aside. Rinse the chicken inside and out with cold water and pat dry with paper towels. Gently stuff the chicken with the Stuffing, then close the cavity with a toothpick or wooden skewer, threading in and out. Wrap the chicken in the lotus leaves, if using, and set aside.
3 To make the Dough, place the flour in a large bowl and gradually add the water while mixing the dough and water together at the same time. When all the water has been added, knead the dough for 2 minutes.
4 Lightly oil a clean surface, then oil your hands and rub over the dough to lightly coat it in oil. Roll the dough into a rectangle, large enough to enclose the chicken. Place the lotus-wrapped chicken in the center of the dough and wrap to enclose the chicken, pinching the seams of the dough to seal.
5 Place the chicken on a baking sheet or roasting pan, and bake in the preheated oven for 3 hours, or until the dough is golden brown. Remove the dough from the chicken and serve the chicken whole at the dining table, with Ginger Garlic Sauce (page 24).

Note: Lotus leaves are very large and sold dried in Chinese markets. They are used for wrapping rice or meats before steaming or baking. If you can't find lotus leaves, you may omit them.

Serves 4–6   Preparation time: 1 hour   Cooking time: 3 hours

Twice-cooked Pork with Peppers   Hui Guo Rou

Sweet red and green peppers add color and a contrasting texture to this quick recipe, where pork is flavored with salted black beans, chili, and hoisin sauce. "Twice-cooked" refers to the use of previously cooked leftover pork, however, fresh meat may be used also. Cooking the pork several times removes all the moisture and gives the meat a distinctive texture.

8 oz (250 g) cooked or uncooked
  pork, thinly sliced
1 tablespoon oil
1 large red bell pepper, sliced
1 large green bell pepper, sliced
2–3 teaspoons chili paste
1 teaspoon hoisin sauce
1 heaped tablespoon salted black
  beans, soaked, drained, and slightly
  mashed
2 cloves garlic, minced
1 tablespoon grated ginger
2 teaspoons soy sauce
2 teaspoons sugar
$1/_4$ teaspoon ground white pepper
1 spring onion, coarsely chopped

1 If using uncooked pork, heat 1 teaspoon of oil in a wok over high heat and lightly stir-fry the pork until it is cooked. Remove the pork from the wok and set aside.
2 Heat the oil in a wok over medium-high heat, then add the peppers and stir-fry for 2 minutes. Add the sliced pork and stir-fry for 1 minute. Remove the pork and peppers from the wok and set it aside aside.
3 Add the chili paste to the wok and stir-fry for 30 seconds, then add the remaining ingredients and stir-fry for 1 minute, mixing thoroughly. Return the pork and peppers to the wok, stir to heat through and serve.

Serves 4   Preparation time: 10 mins   Cooking time: 40 mins

Beef with Black Pepper   Hei Jiao Niu Rou

Simple and quick to prepare, this dish tastes like a flavor-enhanced version of black pepper steak, with Sichuan peppercorns adding a distinctive difference.

1 lb (500 g) beef fillet, trimmed and cut into 1 in (2$^1/_2$ cm) cubes
4 tablespoons rice wine or sake
$^1/_2$ teaspoon salt
$^1/_4$ teaspoon ground white pepper
2 teaspoons oil
4 cloves garlic, minced
2 teaspoons coarsely ground black peppercorns
1 teaspoon crushed Sichuan pepper-corns
4 teaspoons oyster sauce
4 teaspoons soy sauce
2 teaspoons sesame oil
6 lettuce leaves, shredded
2 fresh red chilies, sliced

1 Place the beef in a bowl and add the rice wine, salt, and white pepper. Mix and set aside for 10 minutes.
2 Heat the oil in a wok over high heat and stir-fry the beef until browned on all sides, about 3 minutes. Lower the heat to medium-high, then add the garlic, and stir-fry for 30 seconds. Add the remaining ingredients, except for the lettuce and chilies, and stir-fry for 1 minute, mixing well.
3 Serve the beef on a bed of shredded lettuce, surrounded by slice red chili.

Serves 4   Preparation time: 10 mins   Cooking time: 6 mins

Mongolian Lamb Hotpot Shuan Yang Rou

Paper thin slices of lamb with tofu and cabbage, cooked and seasoned to your liking, followed by a bowl of rice vermicelli in rich stock. This is a cold-weather dish that is said to fortify the blood (it has become popular in Japan also, where it is known as *shabu-shabu*).

1 lb (500 g) boneless leg of lamb
1 lb (500 g) firm tofu, sliced
7 oz (200 g) Chinese cabbage, sliced
4 oz (100 g) dried rice vermicelli, soaked in hot water to soften

Stock
$1^1/_2$ in (4 cm) ginger, sliced
1 spring onion, sliced
2 teaspoons soy sauce
1 teaspoon brown sugar
6 cups ($1^1/_2$ liters) vegetable stock

Dips and Garnishes
Sesame Sauce (page 25)
Soy sauce
Red rice vinegar
Chili oil
Pickled Garlic (page 24)
Chili Garlic Sauce (page 25)
Fresh coriander leaves (cilantro), minced

1 Place all the Stock ingredients in a pot and heat gently over low heat. Transfer the ingredients to a hotpot, steamboat or fondue pot, then bring to a simmer.
2 Arrange the Dips and Garnishes in small bowls and place them on the dining table.
3 Wrap the lamb in plastic wrap and place it in the freezer for 30 minutes. When the lamb is half-frozen, remove the plastic wrap, and with a very sharp knife, slice the lamb across the grain into paper thin slices. Roll up the slices and arrange the slices on a plate. Arrange the tofu and cabbage on separate plates and divide the rice vermicelli among 6 soup bowls.
4 Each diner can cook their own portion of meat, tofu and cabbage in the simmering soup, then season them with the numerous bowls of Dips and Garnishes.
5 When all the lamb, tofu and cabbage have been cooked and eaten, pour the stock over the rice vermicelli, and enjoy as a final course.

Serves 6   Preparation time: 30 mins   Cooking time: 10 mins

Sweet and Sour Pork

This sweet and tangy sauce is best made with Chinese rice vinegar, but distilled cider vinegar will work as well. This recipe makes sweet and sour sauce the traditional way, where the sauce is translucent and thin. Modern versions of this recipe often include a thick sauce and a variety of other vegetables as well. If you desire, you can add carrots, onions, or any other of your vegetable favorites. If canned pineapple is used, the syrup may be substituted for the sugar and water called for in the sauce below.

1 lb (500 g) boneless pork, cut into bite-sized cubes
1 tablespoon cornstarch
Oil for deep-frying
1 tablespoon minced garlic
1 tablespoon minced ginger
1 green or red bell pepper, diced
2 spring onions, sliced into lengths
1 cup (100 g) fresh or canned pineapple chunks (optional)

Batter
$3/_4$ cup (100 g) flour
$3/_4$ cup (100 g) cornstarch
2 teaspoons baking powder
$1/_4$ teaspoon salt
1 cup (250 ml) water
$1^1/_2$ teaspoons oil

Sauce
$1/_2$ cup (125 ml) Chinese white or cider vinegar
$1/_2$ teaspoon salt
2 tablespoons tomato ketchup
1 tablespoon soy sauce
$1/_2$ cup (125 g) sugar
$1^1/_2$ tablespoons cornstarch, blended with $3/_4$ cup (175 ml) water

1 To make the Batter, combine the flour, cornstarch, baking powder, and salt in a large bowl. Gradually pour in the water, mixing with a fork until smooth. Add the oil and mix well. Set aside.

2 Whisk together all the Sauce ingredients and set aside.

3 Combine the pork with the cornstarch. Heat the oil in a wok until it just starts to smoke. Working in small batches, use tongs to dip the pork in the Batter, then into the wok. Deep-fry the pork for a few seconds until it is a light brown, then remove from the wok and drain on paper towels. Use a slotted spoon to discard any batter from the wok. Repeat until all the pork has been battered and fried.

4 Return all the pork to the wok and deep-fry a second time, this time for about 3 minutes, or until golden brown. This step is optional, but it removes the remaining moisture from the pork and makes it crispy and chewy—similar to what you get in a Chinese restaurant. Discard the oil and return the wok to the stove over high heat.

5 Stir-fry the garlic and ginger for 30 seconds, add the bell pepper, and continue to stir-fry for 1 minute. Add the spring onion, pineapple chunks, and Sauce, mix well and bring to a boil. Pour over the pork and serve with rice.

Note: A splatter screen for covering the wok comes in handy when the pork is returned to the pan for additional frying.

Serves 4–6   Preparation time: 20 mins   Cooking time: 30 mins

Beef with Sesame Seeds Zhi Ma Niu Pai

Thin slices of beef are stir-fried quickly, combined with a light sauce, and finished with a generous sprinkling of toasted sesame seeds.

8 oz (250 g) beef fillet
$1/4$ cup (60 ml), plus 2 teaspoons oil
2 cloves garlic, minced
1 tablespoon grated ginger
2 teaspoons cornstarch, blended with 2 teaspoons water
2 tablespoons sesame seeds, lightly toasted

Sauce
1 tablespoon rice wine or sake
1 teaspoon soy sauce
1 teaspoon black vinegar
2 teaspoons sugar
$1/4$ teaspoon ground white pepper
$1/2$ cup (125 ml) chicken stock

1 To make the Sauce, combine the ingredients and set aside.
2 Slice the beef into thin slices, then place the slices on a chopping board and flatten them with the broad side of a cleaver. Heat $1/4$ cup (60 ml) of the oil in wok over high heat and stir-fry the beef slices for 2 to 3 minutes. Drain on a plate lined with paper towels and set aside.
3 Heat the remaining 2 teaspoons of oil over medium-high heat and stir-fry the garlic and ginger for a few seconds. Add the Sauce and mix well.
4 Stir in the cornstarch mixture until the Sauce thickens, then add the beef, coating well with the Sauce. Sprinkle with toasted sesame seeds and serve immediately.

Note: To toast raw sesame seeds, place the sesame seeds in a dry skillet and heat over medium heat. Stir continuously for about 2 to 3 minutes until the seeds are lightly browned and fragrant. Remove and set aside.

Serves 2   Preparation time: 10 mins   Cooking time: 10 mins

Red-braised Fish

Red-braising is a traditional Chinese method of cooking meat, poultry, and seafood. After searing the food in hot oil, a fragrant sauce is poured over, then the pan is covered while the food slowly braises. The characteristic red sheen is produced by the fusion of soy sauce, sugar and fat.

1 lb (500 g) fresh fish steaks or fillets
   (tuna, halibut, seabass, or swordfish)
1 tablespoon oil
2 spring onions, sliced

Sauce
$2^1/_2$ tablespoons soy sauce
$2^1/_2$ tablespoons rice wine or sake
$1^1/_2$ teaspoons sugar
$^1/_2$ teaspoon sesame oil
1 teaspoon vinegar
1 tablespoon shredded ginger
1 tablespoon water
1 tablespoon chili paste (optional)

1 Combine the Sauce ingredients in a bowl, and set aside.
2 Rinse the fish and pat it dry with paper towels. Heat a skillet or wok over medium-high heat. Rub the cooking surface with a piece of freshly cut ginger, then add the oil. When the oil begins to sizzle, add the fish steaks and cook for 2 minutes on each side.
3 Pour the Sauce over the fish and leave covered for 1 to 2 minutes. Turn the fish, add the spring onion and braise for 2 minutes. Serve immediately.

Serves 4   Preparation time: 10 mins   Cooking time: 10 mins

Ginger-seasoned Fish with Carrots, Bamboo Shoots, and Celery

A quick and tasty way to prepare fish; succulent ginger-seasoned morsels of fish are tossed with pieces of tender-crisp carrot and celery.

1 lb (450 g) white fish fillets, thinly sliced
1/2 tablespoon grated ginger
1 small carrot, peeled and sliced
1/2 cup (125 g) bamboo shoots, thinly sliced
1 cup (100 g) celery, sliced on a diagonal
1 tablespoon oil
2 cloves garlic, minced
1/2 teaspoon salt
1 tablespoon soy sauce
1 tablespoon rice wine or sake
1/4 teaspoon sugar
1 tablespoon water
2 spring onions, sliced
Pinch of ground white pepper

1 Combine the fish with the grated ginger and set aside.
2 Refresh all the vegetables by placing them in iced water for a few minutes, then drain and set aside.
3 Heat the oil in a medium-sized skillet or wok until very hot. Add the garlic and stir-fry for 30 seconds, then add the vegetables and continue to stir-fry for 2 minutes.
4 Add the fish to the skillet, stir gently to mix through, then add the salt, soy sauce, rice wine, sugar, and water. Continue to stir for another 2 minutes until the flesh is opaque and the fish is cooked.
5 Toss gently with the spring onion, turn off the heat, and sprinkle with white pepper. Serve with Ginger and Soy Dip (page 25).

Serves 4   Preparation time: 15 mins   Cooking time: 6 mins

Stir-fried Shrimp or Lobster with Chili Sauce

This quick and easy stir-fry can also be made with fresh lobster meat for a wonderful indulgence.

1$^1/_2$ lbs (750 g) large shrimp, peeled and deveined or 8 oz (250 g) fresh lobster meat
1 teaspoon cornstarch, blended with $^1/_4$ cup (60 ml) water
1 egg white
$^1/_2$ teaspoon plus a pinch of sugar
$^1/_2$ teaspoon salt
2 tablespoons oil
$^3/_4$ cup (50 g) snow peas, sliced
4 cloves garlic, minced
$^1/_2$ tablespoon grated ginger
$^1/_2$ tablespoon soy sauce
1 tablespoon rice wine or sake
1 tablespoon chicken stock
$^1/_2$ tablespoon chili bean paste
2 tablespoons tomato ketchup

1 Season the shrimp or lobster with the cornstarch mixture, egg white, $^1/_2$ teaspoon sugar, and $^1/_4$ teaspoon salt. Massage the shrimp or lobster gently, mixing well. Set aside.

2 Heat 1 tablespoon of oil in a wok until very hot, then add the snow peas, $^1/_4$ teaspoon salt, and a pinch of sugar. Stir-fry for 1 minute, then remove from the heat and set aside.

3 Heat the remaining oil in a wok until very hot, then stir-fry the shrimp or lobster for 1 minute. Add the garlic and ginger, stirring to mix thoroughly. Add the soy sauce, rice wine, chicken stock, chili bean paste, and tomato ketchup. Continue to stir-fry until the shrimp or lobster is cooked, then serve.

Serves 4   Preparation time: 15 mins   Cooking time: 10 mins

Shrimp with Vegetables and Ham

Slivered vegetables and ham encircled with shrimp, as in the photograph opposite, resemble the long hair pins that are traditionally pushed through a twist of hair. This dish can also be turned into a simple stir-fry, by cooking the shrimp and vegetables in a bit of oil, and then adding the ingredient for the sauce to the wok at the end.

8 large shrimp, peeled and deveined
$^1/_2$ teaspoon sesame oil
3 spring onions, slivered
1 carrot, peeled and cut into matchsticks
$^1/_2$ cup (100 g) slivered Yunnan or salted Parma ham
1 teaspoon cornstarch, blended with 1 teaspoon water

Sauce
4 tablespoons chicken stock
1 tablespoon rice wine or sake
$^1/_4$ teaspoon salt
1 clove garlic, minced

1 To make the Sauce, combine all the ingredients together and set aside.
2 Flatten the shrimp and drizzle with sesame oil. Use the tip of a sharp knife to slash a hole near the head end of the shrimp, and another hole near the tail end. Take one piece each of spring onion, carrot, and ham and, holding them together, push through one slit of the shrimp. Fold the shrimp into a semi-circle and push the bundle out through the other slit.
3 Fill a wok half full of water and bring to a boil over high heat. Add the shrimp and blanch for 2 minutes, or until they turn opaque. Remove and place on a serving dish.
4 Pour off the water and return the wok to the stove over medium-high heat. Add the Sauce and bring to a boil. Lower the heat to medium and stir in the cornstarch mixture. Pour the Sauce over the shrimp and serve.

Serves 4   Preparation time: 10 mins   Cooking time: 15 mins

Wok-seared Sesame Scallops

Sweet sea scallops infused with the nutty taste of sesame and a hint of ginger.

10 oz (300 g) fresh sea scallops
1 teaspoon oil
2 spring onions, sliced
Sesame seeds, to garnish

Marinade
1 teaspoon sesame oil
1 tablespoon hoisin sauce
$1/_2$ tablespoon soy sauce
1 tablespoon rice vinegar
1 tablespoon grated ginger

1 To make the Marinade, whisk all the ingredients together. Pour the Marinade into a plastic bag and add the scallops. Seal the bag and leave to marinate in the refrigerator for at least 1 hour.

2 Heat 1 teaspoon of oil in a wok over medium-high heat, then add the scallops and spring onions. Cook the scallops for 4 minutes on each side, or until they are opaque. Garnish with sesame seeds.

Serves 2–4   Preparation time: 5 mins + 1 hour marinating time
Cooking time: 8 mins

Steamed Mussels, Clams or Oysters with Garlic

Mussels, clams or oysters can also be used in this simple and tasty recipe. The shellfish are boiled until they just open, then steamed with seasonings and topped with a garnish of fried garlic, spring onion, chili, and fresh coriander leaves. A teaspoon of mashed salted black beans or *miso* may also be sprinkled over the shellfish before final steaming.

2 lbs (1 kg) fresh mussels or clams
  or oysters
8 cloves garlic
1 teaspoon oil
1 teaspoon chicken stock powder or
  $1/2$ chicken bouillon cube, crumbled
1 teaspoon sugar
1 teaspoon soy sauce
1 fresh red chili, minced
1 spring onion, thinly sliced
1 tablespoon minced fresh coriander
  leaves (cilantro)

1 Pick over the shellfish and discard any open shells. Bring a wok of water to a boil over high heat, then add the shellfish and cook until the shells open, about 2 to 3 minutes. Drain and discard any unopened shells. Remove one half of the shell from the mussels, clams, or oysters, and arrange them open-faced in a bamboo steamer. Set aside.
2 Thinly slice four cloves of the garlic. Heat the oil over medium to high heat in a small skillet and fry the sliced garlic until crisp, about 3 minutes. Drain and discard the oil, and set the fried garlic aside.
3 Mince the remaining cloves of garlic and sprinkle it over the mussels or clams or oysters, together with the chicken stock powder, sugar, and soy sauce. Cover and steam over boiling water for 3 minutes.
4 Garnish with the fried garlic, chili, spring onion, and coriander leaves and serve immediately.

Serves 4   Preparation time: 10 mins   Cooking time: 6 mins

Ginger-poached Trout or Seabass

Do not attempt this dish unless you can be sure of absolutely fresh fish as the seasonings are subtle, so the quality of the fish is vital. Perch, cod or pomfret are good substitutes.

1 whole fresh trout or seabass (1$^1/_2$ lbs/700 g), cleaned and deboned, or 1 lb (500 g) fresh fish fillets
3 spring onions, cut into thin strips
4 in (10 cm) ginger, cut into thin strips
1 fresh red chili, deseeded and cut into thin strips
1 tablespoon rice wine or sake
2 tablespoons rice vinegar
$^1/_2$ teaspoon salt
$^1/_4$ teaspoon ground white pepper

1 Place the fish in a wok and add just enough water to cover. Add half the spring onion, half the ginger, and bring to a boil. Reduce the heat and simmer gently until the fish is cooked, about 5 minutes. Remove from the wok and place on a serving plate.
2 Combine the rice wine, vinegar, salt, and pepper and pour over the fish. Garnish with the remaining spring onion, ginger, and chili. Serve immediately.

Serves 2   Preparation time: 5 mins   Cooking time: 5 mins

Sweet Black Bean and Sesame Squid

Squid has long been prized in Chinese kitchens as an excellent yet inexpensive source of protein and essential minerals from the sea. This stir-fried dish is punctuated by fresh red chilies and sweet black bean and sesame sauce.

1 tablespoon oil
4–6 cloves garlic, thinly sliced
1 tablespoon grated ginger
2–3 fresh red chilies, deseeded and minced; or 1$^1/_2$ teaspoons dried chili flakes
12 oz (350 g) fresh squid, cleaned and cut into bite-sized pieces
Fresh sprigs of parsley, coarsely chopped, to garnish

Black Bean and Sesame Sauce
2 teaspoons rice wine or sake
2 teaspoons sesame oil
1 tablespoon soy sauce
1 tablespoon brown sugar
1 tablespoon water
$^1/_2$ tablespoon black bean paste
$^1/_2$ teaspoon sugar

1 Combine the Black Bean and Sesame Sauce ingredients and set aside.
2 Heat the oil in a wok over medium-high heat, add the garlic, and stir-fry for 1 to 2 minutes until golden brown.
3 Add the ginger and chili, stir-fry for 1 minute, then add the squid and the Black Bean and Sesame Sauce. Stir, mix well, and leave to cook for 1 minute. Garnish with fresh parsley and serve.

Serves 4   Preparation time: 20 mins   Cooking time: 5 mins

Salt and Pepper Squid

Crisp, tender squid sprinkled with salt and ground Sichuan peppercorn. This simple recipe makes a great snack or appetizer as well as a main dish. As with all deep-fried foods, this dish is best served hot.

1 lb (500 g) fresh squid, cleaned
1$^1/_2$ tablespoons grated ginger
1$^1/_2$ tablespoons rice wine or sake
1 teaspoon sugar
Oil for deep-frying
Fresh coriander leaves (cilantro), coarsely chopped, to garnish

Salt and Pepper Sichuan Dip
1 teaspoon salt
$^1/_2$ teaspoon ground Sichuan peppercorns or 1 teaspoon ground red pepper

1 To make the Salt and Pepper Sichuan Dip, combine all the ingredients in a small bowl and set aside.
2 Blanch the squid in a pot of boiling water for 30 seconds, then rinse and drain with cold water. Pat the squid dry with paper towels. Combine the grated ginger, rice wine, and sugar in a medium-sized bowl. Add the squid and mix well, then leave to marinate for 30 minutes.
3 Heat the oil in a wok over high heat. Deep-fry the squid for 30 seconds, then remove with a slotted spoon and drain on paper towels. Sprinkle with the Salt and Pepper Sichuan Dip and toss lightly to coat. Garnish with fresh coriander leaves and serve.

Serves 4   Preparation time: 20 mins   Cooking time: 5 mins

Iced Almond Jelly with Lychees

Smooth, sweet almond gelatin paired with the fresh and slightly tart taste of lychees.

³/₄ cup (180 ml) boiling water
¹/₄ cup (60 g) sugar
1 tablespoon unflavored gelatin
  powder
1 cup (250 ml) milk
1 teaspoon almond extract
1 can (11 oz/350g) lychees, in syrup
Shaved ice, to serve

1 Combine the boiling water, sugar, and gelatin in a medium-sized bowl and stir until the sugar and gelatin are completely dissolved.
2 Add the milk and almond extract and stir. Pour the gelatin mixture into a 9 in (12 cm) square pan and refrigerate until set, about 1¹/₂ hours.
3 Cut the jelly into small squares. To serve, place a few lychees with a bit of syrup and shaved ice in a bowl and top with jelly squares.

Serves 4–6   Preparation time: 5 mins   Cooking time: 1¹/₂ hours

Banana Fritters

Sweet bananas that have been lightly battered, fried until golden, and drizzled with honey. An irresistable snack or a sweet ending to a Chinese meal.

7 large firm bananas, or 15 small
  finger bananas, peeled
Oil for deep-frying
Honey (optional)

Batter
1 cup (125 g) flour
2 tablespoons milk
$^3/_4$ tablespoon butter
1 tablespoon superfine (caster) sugar
$^1/_2$ cup (125 ml) water

1 To make the Batter, combine the flour, milk, butter, and sugar. Gradually add the water, mixing thoroughly until a smooth batter is formed.
2 Halve the larger bananas if necessary, then dip all the bananas in the batter, coating well.
3 Heat the oil in a deep saucepan or a small pot until very hot. Test the oil with a wooden chopstick or a dry wooden spoon; if the oil sizzles, it is ready to be used. Deep-fry the bananas, a few at a time, for 3 minutes until browned on all sides. Drain on paper towels and if desired, serve drizzled with honey.

Serves 4–6   Preparation time: 7 mins   Cooking time: 15 mins

Candied Apples

Apples, crisp Asian pears, or even ripe bananas can be used for this delightful dessert. It is important that everything is laid out in preparation so that the final stages of cooking can be done quickly. The photograph opposite shows this recipe using the tiny apples available in many parts of China during summer months.

2 large green apples
Juice of 1 lemon
1 cup (250 ml) oil
Cooking spray

Batter
1 cup (250 g) white flour
2 tablespoons cornstarch
1 teaspoon baking soda
1 egg, lightly beaten
$^1/_2$–$^3/_4$ cup (125–175 ml) water

Syrup
1 cup (250 g) sugar
$^1/_4$ cup (60 ml) water

1 Peel, core and slice the apples into eight wedges. Place the slices in a large bowl and toss with the lemon juice. Set aside.
2 Prepare the Batter by combining the ingredients in a bowl, adding enough water to achieve the consistency of thick cream.
3 To make the Syrup, heat the sugar and water in a small saucepan over medium heat. Once the sugar dissolves, increase the heat to high and bring to a boil without stirring. Continue to boil until the mixture changes to a golden syrup, about 8 to 10 minutes.
4 While the sugar is boiling, fill a large bowl about half way with ice cubes and fill with cold water. Once the sugar has turned to a Syrup, place the saucepan of Syrup in the bowl of iced water for a few seconds to cool. Set the saucepan back on the stove over low heat and keep warm.
5 Heat the oil in a wok over medium-high heat. While the oil is heating, coat a serving dish with cooking spray. Dip slices of apple, a few at a time, into the Batter and deep-fry for about 30 seconds on each side, or until golden brown. Remove the apple slices with a slotted spoon and drain on a plate lined with paper towels.
6 Dip the fried apple slices into the Syrup with kitchen tongs coated with cooking spray. Coat in the Syrup, then drop the slices into the iced water. Remove immediately, then place the slices on the greased serving dish. Repeat until all the slices are fried and candied, then serve.

Note: Once boiling, it is very important not to stir the Syrup until it reaches the appropriate consistency. Stirring will break the sugar crystals and the syrup will not properly set.

Serves 4   Preparation time: 30 mins   Cooking time: 10 mins

Mango Pudding

Puréed mango and a hint of coconut make this a light, tropical dessert.

3 large ripe mangoes (about 3 lbs/1¹/₂ kgs)
1¹/₂ teaspoons gelatin powder
¹/₂ cup (125 ml) cold water
¹/₂ cup (125 ml) hot water
³/₄ cup (180 g) sugar
¹/₂ cup (125 ml) thick coconut milk
¹/₄ cup (60 ml) heavy cream
1 small mango, sliced into wedges, to garnish (optional)

1 Peel the mangoes, then cut the flesh into smaller pieces. Purée the mango in a blender or food processor and set aside.
2 Place the gelatin in a large bowl, add the cold water, and stir to soften. Pour in the hot water and stir until the gelatin dissolves. Add the puréed mango and mix thoroughly.
3 Combine the sugar, coconut milk, and cream in a bowl, stir until the sugar dissolves, then add it to the mango mixture. Stir to mix. Divide the pudding mixture among six ramekins or cups and refrigerate until set, about 2 hours. Top with mango wedges, if using, before serving.

Serves 6   Preparation time: 15 mins   Cooking time: 2 hours

Sweet Rice Dumplings

These soft and chewy dumplings are filled with the crunch of sesame seeds and peanuts and coated with sweet coconut.

Finely shredded sweetened coconut for rolling
6 maraschino cherries, drained and halved

Filling
2 tablespoons sesame seeds
¹/₄ cup (60 g) unsalted roasted peanuts, diced
3 tablespoons sugar

Dough
3 cups (375 g) glutinous rice flour
²/₃ cup (150 ml) boiling water
¹/₂ cup (125 ml) plus 2 tablespoons cold water

1 Heat a skillet over medium heat and dry-roast the sesame seeds for 2 to 3 minutes, shaking the pan, or until the seeds turn golden brown.
2 Combine the Filling ingredients in a bowl and set aside.
3 To make the Dough, place the glutinous rice flour into a medium-sized bowl, add the boiling water and mix until evenly moistened. Add the cold water and mix until the dough comes together to form a ball. Turn the dough out on a lightly floured surface and knead for 5 minutes, or until the dough is smooth and pliable. Cover with a damp towel and leave to rest for 10 minutes. Roll the dough into a long cylinder and cut into 12 pieces. Cover the pieces with the damp towel.
4 Roll a piece of dough into a 4 in (10 cm) circle, keeping the remaining dough covered to prevent them from drying. Place 2 teaspoons of the Filling in the center of the circle, then wrap up to from a smooth ball, pinching the edges of the dough together to seal. Cover with a damp towel while you fill the remaining dough pieces.
5 Line the trays of a bamboo steamer with damp paper towels. Arrange the dumplings in the steamer, leaving a little bit of space between each dumpling, then cover and steam for 10 minutes.
6 Remove the dumplings and roll them in the shredded coconut. Be sure to keep the steamer closed during this step to keep the dumplings moist, so the coconut sticks to the outside.
7 Garnish each dumpling with half a maraschino cherry and serve immediately, or within an hour.

Makes 12 dumplings   Preparation time: 45 mins   Cooking time: 10 mins

Sweet Red Bean Soup with Lotus Seeds

Red bean soup is generally served as a snack in China and is particularly popular with children.

14 oz (420 g) dried azuki beans
2–3 strips fresh or dried orange peel
8$^3/_4$ cups (2 liters) water
$^1/_4$ cup (60 g) boiled lotus seeds
$^1/_2$ cup (125 g) sugar

1 Place the red beans in a strainer and rinse well.
2 Combine the beans, orange peel and water in a pot and bring to a boil. Reduce the heat and simmer for 45 minutes.
3 Add the lotus seeds, simmer for another 45 minutes, then discard the orange peel.
4 Add the sugar and stir until the sugar dissolves. Serve warm.

Serves 6   Preparation time: 5 mins   Cooking time: 1 hour 30 mins

Sweet Red Bean Pancakes

Sweet red bean paste, made from small red azuki beans and available canned from Asian markets, makes a smooth filling in this well known Sichuan recipe. Azuki beans are very nutritional and are highly regarded in traditional Chinese medicine.

1 egg, lightly beaten
$^3/_4$ cup (175 ml) cold water
$^1/_2$ cup (125 g) flour
$^1/_2$ cup (125 ml) oil
6 tablespoons canned sweet red
    bean paste

1 Combine the beaten egg and cold water and whisk until smooth. Place the flour into a bowl, add the egg mixture and whisk until smooth.
2 Brush a medium-sized skillet with a bit of the oil and heat over medium heat. When the skillet is hot, pour in $^1/_3$ of the batter and swirl to make a thin pancake. Cook until the top of the pancake has set, about 2 minutes if the pan is sufficiently hot.
3 Spread 2 tablespoons of the red bean paste in the middle of the pancake. Using a heatproof spatula to lift the edges of the pancake, fold the side of the pancake over the bean paste. Fold over the other side of the pancake, and then the ends, to form a rectangular shape. Repeat with the remaining portions of batter.
4 Heat the remaining oil in a wok over medium-high heat and fry the pancakes until golden, about 4 minutes per side. Remove the pancakes and drain on paper towels. Serve immediately.

Serves 4–6   Preparation time: 5 mins   Cooking time: 20 mins

Measurements and conversions

Measurements in this book are given in volume as far as possible. Teaspoon, tablespoon and cup measurements should be level, not heaped, unless otherwise indicated. Australian readers, please note that the standard Australian measuring spoon is larger than the UK or American spoon by 5 ml, so use $^3/_4$ tablespoon instead of a full tablespoon when following the recipes.

Liquid Conversions

Imperial	Metric	US cups
$^1/_2$ fl oz	15 ml	1 tablespoon
1 fl oz	30 ml	$^1/_8$ cup
2 fl oz	60 ml	$^1/_4$ cup
4 fl oz	125 ml	$^1/_2$ cup
5 fl oz ($^1/_4$ pint)	150 ml	$^2/_3$ cup
6 fl oz	175 ml	$^3/_4$ cup
8 fl oz	250 ml	1 cup
12 fl oz	375 ml	$1^1/_2$ cups
16 fl oz	500 ml	2 cups

Note:
1 UK pint = 20 fl oz
1 US pint = 16 fl oz

Solid Weight Conversions

Imperial	Metric
$^1/_2$ oz	15 g
1 oz	30g
$1^1/_2$ oz	50 g
2 oz	60 g
3 oz	90 g
$3^1/_2$ oz	100 g
4 oz ($^1/_4$ lb)	125 g
5 oz	150 g
6 oz	185 g
7 oz	200 g
8 oz ($^1/_2$ lb)	250 g
9 oz	280 g
10 oz	300 g
16 oz (1 lb)	500 g
32 oz (2 lbs)	1 kg

Oven Temperatures

Heat	Fahrenheit	Centigrade/Celsius	British Gas Mark
Very cool	225	110	$^1/_4$
Cool or slow	275–300	135–150	1–2
Moderate	350	175	4
Hot	425	220	7
Very hot	450	230	8

Index of recipes